ZERO GRAVITY

Activation in hearing God
p130-131

ZERO GRAVITY

Rivera Douthit

Hunley Press

Zero Gravity

Cover design: Animink – Markus Alison
Cover Photo: Joel Stenkvist and Eric Bock
Contributing Editors: Carol McCall and Carole Ann Loebs, and Dana Ward

Hunley Press
A Division of Gonia Global
99 Jackson St. #131
Davidson, NC 28036

Hunter and Haley, my true joy and inspiration, you are absolutely changing the world for the better just by being you. Keep shining. Keep soaring. Keep dreaming.

~Mom

TABLE OF CONTENTS

Introduction

My purpose in writing this book, besides doing what God has asked me to do, is to share the sacred place I have discovered.

Zero Gravity.

Gravity represents the weight that holds us down, the things that entangle us: sin, choices, circumstances, sickness, depression, weakness and wickedness. These are all inevitably tied to life on earth as humans, but hindered and held back is not the way we were meant to live. God created us as sons and daughters to tap into the fullness of an abundant, weight{less} life.

Part of living the fullest life is discovering how to live up higher, above the noise and chaos of the world. I'm reminded of the lyrics to a song from the 1980s, "Love lift us up where we belong, up where the eagles fly on a mountain high." In the realm where heaven meets earth, we see and hear God clearly and take hold of our true identity. We learn to stop listening to voices of comparison, labels and striving. We lay down fear and misunderstanding and take hold of sweet gifts from our Father. Rising above our flesh, we learn to walk in authority over the enemy by the power of the Holy Spirit.

We are on the cusp of revival, or one of the greatest moves of God in the history of the earth! Revival cannot happen corporately until it first happens individually. To have sustainable revival, we must fully discover who we are as sons and daughters and come together in unity as the Body of Christ. We have to know how to live from heavenly places, hearing God's voice and following.

This is an invitation to transformational, supernatural living. My hope as you begin reading is that the Lord prepares and makes ready the soil of your heart to receive His message. I consider myself a communicator of truth more than a writer, so I have gone to great lengths to write with clarity but preserve the way I verbally communicate. I humbly pray that through these words perspectives will shift, and you will live your fullest life to change the world everywhere you step your feet. My heart's desire is for you to know God and discover yourself like never before.

CHAPTER ONE

The Kingdom Of God Is Like

*"Give me one hundred men who fear
nothing but sin and desire nothing but
God, and I care not whether they be
clergyman or laymen, they alone will
shake the gates of Hell and set up the
kingdom of Heaven upon the earth."*
~ John Wesley

JUST A FEW DAYS before Dave passed, he and Helen renewed their wedding vows. In all my years as a critical care nurse, I witnessed a lot of death, including all the elements of what can happen when a person is dying. My friend Helen's story of her husband's passing fascinated me. Dave asked God to let him live long enough to celebrate their 48th wedding anniversary. God honored his request, and he lived supernaturally longer than expected.

Dave had always been obsessed with time, at some points to a fault. So before he passed, to honor him, Helen told him the exact moment in time they had renewed their vows. He mustered up enough energy to say, "Who cares?" Helen was stunned and sort of chuckled. It was the first time in their 48 years of married life Dave didn't care what time it was. Helen knew right then that he was somewhere in a new dimension. He was closer than ever to being face to face with God where time doesn't matter anymore. In eternity there's no clock. Dave had known Jesus for years, but all of a sudden in light of heaven, time? Who cares! In the Spirit realm, the constraints of earthly living fade into the background. In the kingdom everything shifts, and what mattered most, suddenly doesn't matter at all.

The kingdom is a mystery in some ways. It was one of the primary reasons Jesus came, to teach us about the kingdom of God and show us how to live it on earth. We are coming out of what some have referred to as the Church Era. Our focus is moving beyond Sunday school and going through the motions of singing the same three stanzas of the same hymn, week after week. If all we ever get of Jesus is within the four walls of a building one day a week, we're in trouble. He can't be contained there. We don't go to church to do our Christian duty, to check off a list of dos and don'ts. We are the church. We are temples of the living God. We house His Spirit. Everywhere we go, He goes. The kingdom of God is in us. The Body of Christ is the embodiment of God. His anointing and power are made manifest in us.

What is the Kingdom?

My friend sent a message on the morning of October 7, 2016. It read, "Look what God just showed me. Hurricane Matthew hit today, 10/7. Go read Matthew 10:7." I looked it up, and it said, "Go and announce to them that the kingdom of heaven is near."

According to Merriam-Webster's Dictionary, kingdom is:
1) a politically organized community or major territorial unit

having a monarchical form of government headed by a king or queen.

2) the eternal kingship of God: the realm in which God's will is fulfilled.

3) a realm or region in which something is dominant: an area or sphere in which one holds a preeminent position.

If we use this definition, God's kingdom is a governmental organization in another realm, or in a region on earth in which God is King. His children are appointed to hold dominant or distinguished positions under His rule.

One summer I had a dream where I was walking down a dirt road in the dark. I dropped a small, gold earring. When I bent down to try to find it, I unearthed a tall stack of ancient coins of all sizes. I knew they were worth more than money could buy. God had also been having me read Isaiah 45:3,

> *"I will give you hidden treasures, riches stored in secret places, so that you may know that I am the Lord, the God of Israel, who summons you by name."*

What a sweet gift from the Lord to know that in secret, He wants to give us treasures so valuable a price can't be put on them.

My brother had been periodically working on our family tree for a few years. Around the same time as the dream, he finally had a major breakthrough with a line on my mom's side of the family. Her dad, my grandpa, who was the preacher, had ancestors who were royalty. He traced them all the way back through England to France. We had kings and queens for grandparents many generations removed.

This intrigued me. Royalty—the riches hidden in secret places.

According to Pastor Mike Thornton, it's important to try to find out where and who we're from. It gives insight into the God-given calling on our entire family line for generations. In our particular family, we can see that there is a governmental, leadership, priestly (pastoral) anointing for hundreds of years. We get to ask God to restore to us in this generation the things lost along the way to allow our generation to take back the family blessings and walk in them. Whatever had been written in the story of our lives before we were born, we can ask Him for insight to receive those blessings and live them. Let us be the ones who take back what's been stolen and live out our destiny.

More important than these findings about my earthly family is that I belong to a heavenly kingdom that is everlasting, one that can't be shaken. I'm royalty in God's kingdom, and to me that's the richest treasure of all. The God of creation takes time to sit and talk to me. He delights in me. That's richer than all the money in the world.

A generous friend allowed me to stay in her beachfront property while writing. This was one of the ways God confirmed He wanted me to write this book. This place was so beautifully decorated, and most days I wrote with the door open. The ocean breeze, the sound of crashing waves, and view were spectacular. The first night as I settled in, I was chatting with a friend. I told her I felt like a princess. She said, "You are a princess."

I know I'm a daughter of the King. I get it. But it's easy to forget. The next morning, I spent time with God before I started writing again. That particular morning He took me to Psalm 45.

> *"All glorious is the princess within her chamber; her gown is interwoven with gold. In embroidered garments she is led to the king; her virgin companions follow her—those brought to*

be with her. Led in with joy and gladness, they enter the palace of the king." (verses 13-15)

How sweet. Confirmation. I AM His princess. Then I read this next:

"My heart is stirred by a noble theme as I recite my verses for the king; my tongue is the pen of a skillful writer." (verse 1)

I don't know why this always floors me when it happens. Every time I see God and hear Him clearly it's as exciting as the first time. This time it was confirmation that I am to speak and write as the pen of a skillful writer the words of the Lord. I was moved to tears. Intimacy with God is the richest treasure in the entire world. To be invited into the palace with our King. To be seen, loved and affirmed by Him. He wants to do that with all of us. He's readying His Bride and adorning her with riches in the secret place.

Esther's Preparation

Though there is no mention of God in Esther's story, her life is a picture of His kingdom. Exemplifying true beauty, humility, and preparation of the bride to be presented to her king, her story foreshadows end times. We are living in the days when the Bride (the church) is being prepared and made ready for her coming King. The beginning of the end days was at Pentecost. Anything from that time forward is considered the end days. Esther's life represents the preparation, acceptance, favor, beauty, and authority of the Bride of Christ. As we take a look at her story in chapter 2 of the book of Esther, we see that Esther went through an entire year of preparation before she was ever presented to the king.

"Each young woman's turn came to go in to King Ahasuerus after she had completed twelve months' preparation, according

13

to the regulations for the women, for thus were the days of their preparation apportioned: six months with oil of myrrh, and six months with perfumes and preparations for beautifying women. Thus prepared, each young woman went to the king, and she was given whatever she desired to take with her from the women's quarters to the king's palace." (verses 12-13)

In the quiet, secret place, she waited and prepared. This was a time of cleansing, refining, and purifying with beauty treatments. Esther developed into an even more beautiful woman in this secret place. I believe she found contentment there, making the most of a rather odd situation. This young Jewish woman who had never seen a man in a sexual way was now removed from her family and everything familiar. She was placed in a palace, hidden away, and all of her time for that entire year was devoted to resting, soaking, eating healthy food, making new friends, and no doubt learning the language of royalty.

Preparation is a labor of love and cultivates honor. Even though she didn't know him, Esther's preparation to be presentable to the king was a way of honoring him. Remember the women who prepared spices to take to Jesus' tomb after His death on the cross? They prepared those spices and woke up at the crack of dawn to take them to His tomb, because they loved Him. Nothing speaks love and value to people like being prepared. When we go into situations prepared, we value the time of the other person. We honor God when He asks us to do something and we prepare for it.

Hidden seasons are some of the most beautiful times of revelation. In that place we get to see God and be seen by Him in the most intimate ways. The Bride is becoming more aware of herself and God in this season. She's receiving her healing and purification. She's waking up to her identity. She's realizing her access to everything in the kingdom. I truly believe we are living in a time of increased awareness of God's presence and the vast riches hidden in Christ. If she will bow low in this preparation process, her humility will give her favor with God and man, and an audience with the King.

> *"Esther also was taken to the king's palace, into the care of Hegai the custodian of the women. Now the young woman pleased him, and she obtained his favor; so he readily gave beauty preparations to her, besides her allowance. Then seven choice maidservants were provided for her from the king's palace, and he moved her and her maidservants to the best place in the house of the women." (verses 8-9)*

> *"Now when the turn came for Esther...to go in to the king, she requested nothing but what Hegai the king's eunuch, the custodian of the women, advised. And Esther obtained favor in the sight of all who saw her." (verse 15)*

So Esther wasn't a diva. As noted in the text, she did not request anything unless Hegai advised it. She was humble yet confident. That seems like an oxymoron, but it's possible to be both. Actually we can't truly have one without the other. Humility is a product of true confidence, of knowing who we are by knowing whose we are. Esther knew she was beautiful the way God made her. She knew she didn't need a lot of extra makeup and jewelry to be beautiful. She knew her value and that her beauty was from within.

God, help us become women in this day who will do things when no one is looking and not expect accolades. May we become women who take care of a sick husband or aging parents without complaining, ones who cook or clean for a friend in need without announcing it to the world afterward because we're so starved for affirmation. Help us become laid down lovers of Jesus who are willing to get low. Ones who don't feel the need to give their resume, or be important in the world's eyes. If we want to be like Jesus and represent Him, we have to become poured out vessels empty of ourselves.

God is looking at our hearts, not our outward appearance or our performance. His choosing us has nothing to do with how well we perform. We can't be good enough or beautiful enough for Him to love us more. We can't be bad enough for Him to love us less. He loves us to the max. His love is extravagant. We are chosen because we belong to Him. We're His children.

To see and participate in the next great move of God that is already upon us, humility is a requirement. We will have to be willing to let everything the Spirit wants to do through us be about God and not about us. Everything has to be for His glory and have His name on it.

> *"If you've gotten anything at all out of following Christ, if his love has made any difference in your life, if being in a community of the Spirit means anything to you, if you have a heart, if you care—then do me a favor: Agree with each other, love each other, be deep-spirited friends. Don't push your way to the front; don't sweet-talk your way to the top. Put yourself aside, and help others get ahead. Don't be obsessed with getting your own advantage. Forget yourselves long enough to lend a helping hand." Philippians 2:1-4 (MSG)*

His Bride is in a time of preparation to be presentable. Isn't it lovely to think about the joy our Father will have when He presents an unblemished Bride back to His Son? His Son alone paid the price to make her presentable. Think about it, a wedding where God the Father will present us (the Bride) to the Groom. Beautiful.

Let us lay aside our differences, entering His gates with thanksgiving and His courts with praise. May we honor Him with our willingness to humble ourselves in preparation for the soon and coming King.

The Kingdom of Heaven

Matthew 25 is a kingdom picture on display. *Jesus said, "The kingdom of heaven shall be likened to ten virgins who took their lamps and went out to meet the bridegroom" (verse 1).*

The ten virgins, or bridesmaids, had lamps, which were to be ready when the groom came for his bride. It was custom that these bridesmaids go into the street to meet with the groom. Their lamps were to give light to their path and make way for the coming groom. In this parable Jesus says five of these bridesmaids were wise. They had oil in their lamps and were prepared for the coming groom. The other five foolish virgins were unprepared as their lamps had little oil. They appeared ready outwardly, but it was not lasting. The oil in their lamps burned out, and they missed the coming of the groom.

Jesus was warning that in the last days we must be prepared for His return. Throughout the Bible, oil is symbolic of the Spirit of God. Our lamps must be continually filled. We have to know Him and be filled with His Spirit. It's not enough to be a bridesmaid and have a lamp. Going through the rituals of church, religion and knowing of Jesus aren't enough. We have to know Him intimately by His Spirit. We get to prepare the way of the coming Groom with lamps filled with His oil.

Jesus goes on to share, *"The kingdom of heaven is like a man traveling to a far country, who called out his own servants and delivered his goods to them" (verse 14).* The man gave his servants talents, or money, according to their individual abilities. Two of the servants invested and doubled their money. When the man returned, he said to them, *"Well done, good and faithful servant; you have been faithful over a few things, I will make you ruler over many things. Enter into the joy of your lord."* Upon his return, the man was not pleased with the servant

17

who had not invested, or stewarded, what he had been given. He cast the unprofitable servant into outer darkness.

> *"Then Jesus said, 'When the Son of Man comes in His glory, and all the holy angels with Him, then He will sit on the throne of His glory. All the nations will be gathered before Him, and He will separate them one from another, as a shepherd divides his sheep from the goats.'" (verses 31-32)*

Then those "sheep" seated at his right hand will be given the kingdom prepared for them from the foundation of the world.

The kingdom of heaven is near. Jesus' return is near. It's time to be aware and be prepared. It's time to awaken as a Bride to the preparation season. May we be like Esther, so prepared and confident, we are ready to stand before our King. Let's keep our lamps continually filled with the precious oil of the Spirit, so we will be ready to go out into the highway to make way for the Groom to come in. May we steward all that He's given us to invest with Godly wisdom. May we make time for the one in front of us in line at the store who may need some money or an encouraging word. May we be not just hearers only but doers of the Word. The kingdom of God is like...the least becoming great, leaders being servants, believing like children, and making heavenly investments. It's relationship over religion.

Kingdom mindedness is opposite of the world. Gideon downsized his army for success. A day is as a thousand years, and a thousand years as a day to God. Seven loaves of bread fed 4,000 and then there were seven baskets overflowing with leftovers. In the kingdom, battles of thousands are won with a few, time and space are of no essence, and multitudes are fed to the full with more than plenty in the basket in the end. The world says if we save more, we'll have more. In kingdom economy, the more we give the more we'll have. We have

18

the resources of heaven at our fingertips, because we belong to our Father. We can't out-give God. Generosity is one of the keys to having more than enough. What the world calls wisdom, God calls foolishness.

> *"For the wisdom of this world is foolishness in God's sight."* 1 *Corinthians 3:19*

The Kingdom is about the small things becoming great, and great becoming small. It's about buying fields to find hidden treasure. God's Kingdom is giving up everything for what we know is there but can't see with our earthly eyes. It's seeing beyond the earth with the vision of heaven. Kingdom living is becoming more like Jesus and yielding our hearts and minds to His Spirit. It's hearing the Father and doing what He says. It's believing and living like the power of the resurrection is alive inside of us, because it is.

On Earth As It Is In Heaven

Jesus showed the disciples just how close heaven really is when He demonstrated to them how to pray:

> *"Our Father in heaven, Hallowed be Your name. Your kingdom come. Your will be done on earth as it is in heaven."* *Matthew 6:9-10*

How many times have we stood in church and repeated these words without ever considering what they actually mean? These words alone could change the way we approach God. To address God as Father and hallowed, Holy. Then to ask Him to let His will in heaven come to earth.

"Your kingdom come, Your will be done on earth as it is in heaven."

Jesus taught us to call forth His will in heaven to earth, receiving our heavenly inheritance as His children now. Eternal life, starting now. Living life to the fullest now. Living the will of heaven now. Asking God what's happening now in heaven, then decreeing, "Let it be on earth, Lord."

If we will begin to approach God with this mindset, our lives will be changed. God wants us to experience His goodness and the riches of His storehouse while we're on earth. I'm not talking about a name it, claim it mentality. Our wants need to align with His heart and His desires for us. I'm talking about realizing who He is, who we are, and what we have access to. I do believe there's a vast heavenly supply that we've never experienced here on earth because we didn't know we could.

Reinhard Bonnke says, "We are agents of omnipotence. This means that unlimited power is at our fingertips. It also means that there are no great men working in God's Kingdom. Rather, there is a great God at work in human beings who have childlike faith."

God is doing a new thing. He's readying His Bride. He's taking us from doctrine to relationship. We're moving into the Kingdom Era, a time when the church at large is finding herself. She desires more intimacy with her King. She wants to be presentable to Him. She's ready to get outside the four walls of the building for an adventure with her Love into the highways and byways. She's ready to invite people to the wedding banquet. She wants to use her hands and feet to go, to get her hands dirty, to love people and show them Jesus. Let's not be a people who just "Amen" the worship, the message, and the Bible. May we become it and let it become us.

> *"Therefore, since we are receiving a kingdom that cannot be shaken, let us be thankful, and so worship God acceptably with reverence and awe, for our 'God is a consuming fire.'" Hebrews 12:29*

Prayer:

Jesus, Thank you for setting an example for us so we would know how to walk in love. Thank you for coming to this earthly sod to demonstrate the kingdom to us. Help us to boldly yet gently represent you and your kingdom to others by the power of your Spirit. Amen.

Seated In Heavenly Places

*"Do not fear, little flock, for it is your
Father's good pleasure to give you the
kingdom."*
~ *Luke 12:32*

JENN WAS IN THE seventh month of a perfect pregnancy when she awoke at midnight knowing something was wrong. After an emergency C-section, and many tests, the doctors told Jenn and her husband that their baby boy had no brain function. He could stay alive as long as they kept him on life support. On their fourth day in the neonatal intensive care unit, Ken finally had the chance to hold their son. Ken fell asleep within moments in total peace. As Jenn prayed, wept and contemplated their situation once again, she looked up at her small family and caught a glimpse of God's love. She was reminded of how our heavenly Father had given up His only Son to open up the way of reconciliation to the world.

The next day they knew it was time to let go. As Kael took his last breath, the Spirit of God flooded the room and his parents discovered that they were smiling through the tears. The peace that truly surpasses understanding had filled their hearts and drawn them into a revelation of the goodness of God! Their tragic loss had given them new eyes, and an immediate shift in perspective occurred. They suddenly saw that God does not love us based on what we deserve, but that He actually IS love and gives freely of Himself to all. Everything hinges on revelation of the Father's love. If we don't understand His love, we'll be left believing a lie about who He is and who we are. We will run and strive and hide, attempting to fill up with what never satisfies.

Without knowing His love, we don't know ourselves. Unbeknownst to us, most of our energy is spent trying to identify who we really are, which is why so many people are never quite content. We model ourselves after our version of who we'd like to be through comparison, rather than being satisfied with looking like our Father. We exhaust ourselves as we compare, admire, desire, and mimic to work up a cheap rendition of someone else. Meanwhile, the real us is left to be seen.

Imagine if the whole world knew how loved they are by their heavenly Father? If they could only have eyes to see themselves through His eyes, they would know how adored they really are. If they could wrap their minds around the fact that He loves better than any earthly daddy at his very best. What if they realized the sacrifice He gave of His Son to bring many more sons and daughters, namely them, home.

In the Beginning and Frequently Asked Questions

Let's start at the very beginning, a very good place to start. When you read you begin with ABC. When you sing you begin with do re mi. Do re mi. The first three notes just happen to be...do re mi. Do re mi fa so la ti. I guess every good book needs a little Rodgers and Hammerstein. We watched it every Thanksgiving with my mom's family. The boys would watch football, and the girls would gather to watch the "Sound of Music." Anyway, I digress. The beginning really is a good place to start. It gives clarity to the rest of the story.

Ever wonder what it was like in the beginning? In the beginning, God... What was God thinking? After He created the heavens and the earth, the earth was without form, and void. God was working with a blank slate. It was still dark. Imagine that! No light whatsoever, just pitch-black darkness. God began to speak what He was thinking. Then there were heavens, water and dry land, trees and grass, day and night, sea creatures, birds, and land animals. These were the very thoughts of God put on display. All of these were good according to God. Then He created man, and it was very good.

God created the earth with purpose and order out of the supply of His own mind and heart. The Spirit of God hovered over the face of the waters. God spoke and nothing became something. When God created, His thoughts and words came into existence. What He created was perfect, because it came out of Him and from Him. God makes no mistakes. Through His creation, Adam witnessed what was on God's mind and the perfection of heaven. Earth was a mere reflection of things above, because it was created through the heart, mind, eyes and mouth of God, who created them both.

Where Was Jesus?

Jesus was there in the beginning. He witnessed it all. I imagine since He was the Word who became flesh, He spoke a few Himself.

"Then God said, 'Let Us (Father, Son, Holy Spirit) make man in

25

Our image, according to Our likeness; let them have dominion over the fish of the sea, over the birds of the air, and over the cattle, over all the earth and over every creeping thing that creeps on the earth.' So God created man in His own image; in the image of God He created him; male and female He created them." Genesis 1:26-27

"In the beginning was Word. The Word was with God and the Word was God. He was in the beginning with God." John 1:1-2

How did Satan come into this picture? He was cast out of heaven and down to earth because of pride. God created him with beauty and perfection until iniquity was found in him. He wanted to be worshipped. Satan is where sin originated.

"Your heart was lifted up because of your beauty; You corrupted your wisdom for the sake of your splendor; I (God) cast you to the ground." Ezekiel 28:17a

Satan's given name in heaven was Lucifer, and God seated him above all the other angels until he sinned. You see, God saw what was in his heart and that it wasn't good. God is concerned with our hearts. Jesus said he saw Satan fall like lightning. We are uncertain of the timing of his fall, but we know it was before he met with Eve in the Garden of Eden.

"You were the anointed cherub who covers; I established you; You were on the holy mountain of God; You walked back and forth in the midst of fiery stones. You were perfect in your ways from the day you were created. Till iniquity was found in you. By the abundance of your trading You became filled with violence within, And you sinned; Therefore I cast you as a profane thing Out of the mountain of God." Ezekiel 28:12-19

In the garden, he tempted Eve to eat of the tree of the knowledge of good and evil. There's always dysfunction, disorder, and chaos where Satan and his demons are found. He's constantly offering up counterfeits for what God originally intended. Because he wanted to overthrow God, he was put in his place...low and cast out. God puts things in divine order and gives His glory to no one, so He expelled Satan and his army of fallen angel followers. Satan hates anything about God or resembling Him, including His children. Thus the battle began: good versus evil, light versus darkness, right versus wrong.

Why Humans?

God created humans for several reasons: relationship and family, to give us dominion over the earth, and so we could ultimately reflect and glorify God in all we do. He created us to look, act, and think like Him. Adam woke up in the exact image of God. *"Let Us make man in Our image, according to Our likeness." (Genesis 1:26a)* God, who is Spirit, came to earth and took dust to form man. His breath was released into this dusty formation, and the man came to be. Adam was given a spirit like God's. He communicated with God, spirit to Spirit. Man's original design was the very essence of God wrapped in flesh. God made us to dwell on earth, but we were created with a heavenly DNA and perspective. He put us in the world but we were not of it.

God made a helper for Adam and He created that helper by starting with one of Adam's ribs. She was made with the exact DNA as the man. God breathed in her the same way He did Adam. The two came together to make one. Together, they encompassed the nature of God. Man's heart and woman's heart as one were made to reflect God's heart.

Unfortunately they were introduced to deceit when the serpent slithered his way in and convinced Eve to eat from the only tree in the garden God had warned against. Satan twisted God's words, which he's quite good at doing. She fell for the lie. Adam fell with her. When they sinned, they knew they were naked. After they ate the forbidden fruit, they experienced shame and embarrassment for the first time. They saw their nakedness.

When God created man and released his Spirit on the inside of him, Adam was more aware of his own spirit. Adam and Eve didn't have to wear clothes in the beginning; they wore the glory of God. They were so filled with life and Spirit and were so connected in spirit, that they had no self awareness of skin or their flesh. Sin changed everything, and they became aware of flesh. They hid and covered themselves.

My friend, Allyson, always tells her daughter before she heads off to college, "Don't forget who you are." What she's saying is "Remember what we've taught you. Remember where you came from. Don't forget who you belong to. Don't forget who you're representing." Adam had a momentary memory lapse and forgot where he had come from and who he was representing. Adam lost intimate fellowship with God that day. He experienced death to his spirit. His peace and joy were diminished. He began to see through eyes of sickness, hopelessness, and deceit. His identity and destiny were derailed by bad choices. He forgot who he was. He forgot whose he was.

Adam and Eve were now fleshly and carnal. They were no longer in perfect fellowship with God nor submitted to His Spirit. Adam was no longer living from the Spirit-DNA of his original design. Living from his soul, he fell into sin—lying and hiding. It became his new nature. Now he was spending his days being someone he wasn't meant to be. Adam and Eve hid because they were fearful and ashamed. It was the beginning of humans navigating life with a sin nature, being led by their flesh rather than the Spirit.

Who Am I?

My brother hated being youngest in school. Seemingly he couldn't be Keith; most deemed him "Rivera's brother." When my children were young, I lost my name too. I became "mom." People are trying so desperately to figure out who they are. We need to be identified with something.

Many are labeled with diagnoses, titles, careers, and accomplishments. Identity is who we are, not what we do. They may be closely related. We may do what we do because of who we are, but we are not who we are because of what we do.

We are children of God.

> *"For as many as are led by the Spirit of God, these are sons of God. For you did not receive the spirit of bondage again to fear, but you received the Spirit of adoption by whom we cry out, 'Abba, Father.' The Spirit Himself bears witness with our spirit that we are children of God, and if children, then heirs—heirs of God and joint heirs with Christ, if indeed we suffer with Him, that we may also be glorified together." Romans 8:14-17*

The Trinity: Father, Son and Holy Spirit are a family. God encompasses family in perfection. Our earthly families were created to be public representations of heaven's family. Unfortunately, there's a war raging to cause division, deception and destruction to families. If Satan destroys family, he has attempted to win by targeting what God values most.

In the beginning, God created Adam and Eve to establish humans as part of His family. Unfortunately with sin, the freedom to choose was ushered in. Now we have to decide whether we will allow Him to Father us. When Jesus taught the disciples to pray, He said, "Our Father." He didn't say, "My Father." He was telling us we can call Him Father too. We can be family.

Some people were raised in difficult circumstances and have a skewed view of family, or what a father or mother should be. Our identity isn't from our earthly parents. God used them to get us here. He tells us to honor them. They've made mistakes, as we all have. We need to forgive them. Don't forget, we came from God, and He perfectly encompasses the father and mother's heart for us. His thoughts about us are perfect. *"Before I formed you, I knew you." (Jeremiah 1:5a)* We were known and loved by God before our parents ever thought about us. He knew us before He created us.

Even with their faults, most earthly fathers and mothers who truly love their children still give good gifts to them.

> *"If you then, being evil, know how to give good gifts to your children, how much more will your Father who is in heaven give good things to those who ask Him!" Matthew 7:11*

Our heavenly Father has this gift-giving thing mastered! Don't think for a minute He couldn't possibly love you this way. Of course He could. He does. He proved it by giving us His most valuable possession, His beloved Son. God giving us His very best is not dependent upon us being our very best. He's not a Father who favors one child over another based on performance, though He does see our hearts. His affections are equally distributed in that we are each and every one His favorite. Not only does our Father give good gifts, but also He gives the Holy Spirit to those who ask. He gives gifts of divine design, gifts only He can give.

"If you then, being evil, know how to give good gifts to your children, how much more will your heavenly Father give the Holy Spirit to those who ask Him!" Luke 11:13

Referring to the Holy Spirit, Jesus said: *"If you love Me, keep My commandments. And I will pray the Father, and He will give you another Helper, that He may abide with you forever—the Spirit of truth, whom the world cannot receive, because it neither sees Him nor knows Him; but you know Him, for He dwells with you and will be in you. I will not leave you orphans; I will come to you." John 14:15-18*

Remember that those led by the Spirit of God are sons of God (Romans 8:14). Jesus promised not to leave us orphaned. He said He would come to us, but until then, He's sent us His Spirit. As His children, we can have our Father's promises and gifts by way of His Spirit. The Spirit life is the fullest life. How full? Let's see. Ephesians 1 says we're blessed with every spiritual blessing. Not just a few spiritual blessings. It says every spiritual blessing. That's massive! If we stopped there, it would seem to be enough. But the list goes on. We're chosen, holy, blameless, adopted, accepted in the Beloved, forgiven, heirs (given an inheritance), saved, and sealed with a Holy Spirit deposit with the promise of more to come. That's a stout list of promise and identity as God's children.

Here's even more:
Colossians 1:13-14 (forgiven)
2 Corinthians 5:21 (righteous, made right)
Ephesians 3:20 (empowered by His Spirit)
John 1:12 (child of God)
Romans 5:1 (justified, and have peace with God)
Romans 8:31, 37 (confident conqueror)

My ministry friend, Mike Thornton, challenged me in the last year to

31

ask God who I am, on a deeper level. He encouraged me to ask God who He created me to be, beyond the obvious. As I spent time asking God, I was surprised by some of His answers. They were not assignments. They were more like God given titles. For example, He showed me I'm a spiritual mother. He confirmed this through His Word. Spiritual mother isn't an assignment, it's part of God's specific DNA for me. It's identity. I'm identified with it in heaven. Now, I can choose to accept it and walk it out, or not.

Most of us know we're His children, and we know what that involves. Now at least we know we're all the things listed above that go along with being His child. Who we are and the destiny we've been given is our inheritance as sons and daughters of God. Who does He say you are? Ask Him. You may be surprised. After realizing our spiritual DNA, we can begin asking God what assignments He might want to give us to correlate with who we are. Identity is key to being catapulted into destiny.

Jesus

Through Jenn and Ken's loss of their first baby, they gained clarity. They received their heavenly vision. As God would have it, they now have two beautiful children on earth and one in heaven. Jenn had dreamed of having an all-natural home birth. Ken had the privilege to help Jenn deliver their new baby boy, alive and well, last year, in the privacy of their home. What a picture of the redeeming love of the Father. Sometimes we have to get our sight restored, but He sure turns things around for His children, giving us the deepest desires of our hearts.

Isn't that just like what the Father did for us with Jesus? He delivered Jesus from death to make all things alive and well. Through Jesus things were set back in order. Everything we believe as Christians hinges on the resurrection of Jesus. Life. Abundant life. Without it, nothing else would matter. Jesus is the will of God made manifest. Jesus is God's heart. God sent Him to restore all that was lost, to redeem and to fix what we screwed up. Jesus was no ordinary man. Jesus is the perfect display of the Father in human flesh; He's the super to our natural. He came to give us back our divine design. To restore our identity and inheritance, He got low with us. He didn't have to, but He did.

> *"(Jesus) Who, being in very nature God, did not consider equality with God something to be used to his own advantage; rather, he made himself nothing by taking the very nature of a servant, being made in human likeness. And being found in appearance as a man, he humbled himself by becoming obedient to death—even death on a cross!" Philippians 2:6-8 (NIV)*

Because Jesus came down, we get to go up.

> *"But God, who is rich in mercy, because of His great love with which He loved us, even when we were dead in trespasses, made us alive together with Christ (by grace you have been saved), and raised us up together, and made us sit together in the heavenly places in Christ Jesus." Ephesians 2:4-6*

Because of Jesus, we've been raised up to sit together in heavenly places. Sound familiar? We sit above the chaos, in a higher dimension. From the place of our original design, up in heavenly places in the Spirit realm, we're seated in His presence and given His perspective. Communing with Him spirit to Spirit, the earthly noise fades.

In Revelation 4, John heard a voice like a trumpet say, *"'Come up here, and I will show you things which must take place after this.' Immediately*

I was in the Spirit; and behold, a throne set in heaven, and One sat on the throne." John was in the Spirit, seeing the throne of God and One seated in all His splendor. He was invited to come up, to get closer and see from God's perspective. He was invited to see what God sees. He got a front row seat to things above.

Jesus. Oh to taste and see His goodness and have Him revealed in purity and truth. Jesus said, *"Anyone who has seen me has seen the Father."* *(John 14:9b)* Ask the Holy Spirit to reveal Jesus in new ways. As we glimpse Him, we've glimpsed our Father.

> *"And now, O Father, glorify Me together with Yourself, with the glory which I had with You before the world was." John 17:5*

Jesus didn't come in all HIs glory. He laid down His God power, yet He never sinned. The Spirit of God led Him. At 30 years old, He was baptized. The Spirit fell on Him. And God said, *"This is my beloved Son, in whom I'm well pleased." (Matthew 3:17)* From that moment, Jesus walked in the anointing of the Spirit. If He came in the glory of God, He would not have needed anointing. Jesus came as a man. He was One with the Father in Spirit. He showed us what that looks like. He came to demonstrate to us sonship and reintroduce us to our true identity.

Jesus made a way for us to be forgiven. He didn't come to give us a good message to preach, He came to give us one to live. He showed us what we've been put here to do. He was a man. He was THE Man. He modeled what it looks like to be a real man. He wanted the disciples to learn to do what He was doing. Jesus said:

> *"Most assuredly, I say to you, he who believes in Me, the works that I do he will do also; and greater works than these he will do, because I go to My Father." John 14:12*

Jesus gave us the keys to walk in the identity and authority we were originally given in the garden. The enemy had stolen it from our possession. Jesus took it back. He came to defeat death on the cross to win the victory over sin. Jesus taught us how to have dominion, how to rule and reign on earth over all the power of the enemy.

Romans 8 says creation is eagerly awaiting, even groaning, to see the manifestation (or the revealing) of the sons and daughters of God. Creation is anticipating us rising up to be who God created us to be and live out our destinies. All of heaven and earth are waiting for us to rule and reign as sons and daughters of the King of kings. As God's children, we have a heavenly inheritance. We've been destined to greatness and given authority over the enemy by the Spirit of God Himself.

This is our potential. We were created to walk in the Spirit and dwell on earth. Instead, We are mostly walking in a fleshly existence. We were created for more than we can imagine. Just as we have mannerisms like our earthly parents, the more we get to know our Father, the more our mannerisms resemble His. The more we know Him, the more we'll know ourselves. His Spirit in us will cause us to naturally begin to think, act and look like Him.

> *"And so it is written, 'The first man Adam became a living being.' The last Adam became a life-giving spirit. However, the spiritual is not first, but the natural, and afterward the spiritual. The first man was of the earth, made of dust; the second Man is the Lord from heaven. As was the man of dust, so also are those who are made of dust; and as is the heavenly Man, so also are those who are heavenly. And as we have borne the image of the man of dust, we shall also bear the image of the heavenly Man."* 1 Corinthians 15:45-49

We were supposed to come into the earth as supernatural beings, but when Adam sinned, He became lifeless and spiritually emaciated. He lost heavenly perspective and eternal life, which isn't something we only get when we go to heaven. It is something we are given when we believe in Jesus as the Son of God who came to save us. Eternal life starts now. His limitless, Spirit-filled life is here for the taking. We can experience it right away, even while we're walking in our mortal bodies.

We shall bear the image of the heavenly Man. Instead of complaining about the things holding us back, we can get up with God, above the noise and chaos of sin splattered earth. There we can live untangled and free—zero gravity. Come up with Him in heavenly places, taste and see His goodness, and see the world from His perspective.

Prayer:
Father, Thank you for our heavenly inheritance. Help us to see you for who you really are and receive our rich inheritance as your sons and daughters. Help us believe you when you whisper the truth of who we are and just how delighted you are with us as your children. Thank you for the authority we've been given to rule and reign with you on this earth by the power of your Holy Spirit. In Jesus' name. Amen.

CHAPTER THREE

Color Of Love

"At the end of the day, people won't remember what you said or did, but they will remember how you made them feel."
~ *Maya Angelou*

MY DAUGHTER AND I were shopping in a local supermarket. As the cashier was scanning my items, I felt God say, "I want you to pay for the items of the woman behind you. Whatever she's purchasing, have the cashier ring it up before you leave."

The backstory to this is that racial tension had been rising due to riots in Ferguson, Missouri. During that time, you could feel the tension just standing in line at the grocery store. I remember one day when I said "black," referring to the color of a shirt. A woman near me in line turned and looked as if I was referring to her personally. During those weeks, when Ferguson was the only story in the news, the term black was like speaking a curse word here in the South. Everybody was on edge and the spirit of offense was tangible. Another part of the backstory is that the Lord had been teaching me about the power of giving. We can't out give Him. All the resources in heaven and earth belong to Him. I'm His daughter and have access to all that belongs to Him. Of course, this doesn't mean I can spend carelessly. It does mean if He asks me to give generously, I can trust He will provide all my needs and then some.

I hadn't looked to see if there was a "woman" standing behind me. God had said to pay for the woman's items. Sure enough when I turned around, an older African American woman was in line with a few items in her arms. I quietly told the cashier to include the items for the woman behind me with my purchase. As the cashier scanned the items, the woman said, "No. Wait a minute. These are mine."

The cashier got excited to be in on the blessing. She smiled and said, "I know. This lady asked me to add your items to hers so she could pay for them."

The woman looked completely stunned. She said, "What? Really?" Looking at me with confusion, she asked, "Why?"

I smiled and said, "Jesus loves you, and He wanted me to bless you."

I gathered my bags to leave. She followed. She grabbed me and hugged my neck. Looking directly into my eyes, with tears in hers, she said, "I raised 12 children as a single mom. I did it all by myself. Nobody ever did a single thing to help me in all those years, until today. Thank you! You will never know what this means to me. This is the first time anybody ever did anything to help me."

I said, "Well God wants you to know He sees you and loves you. He knows what you've been through and hasn't forgotten you." I felt something happening spiritually in that moment. God was shifting her heart toward Him, and changing wrong mindsets about color. I knew she genuinely felt loved as she saw God caring and providing for her in that moment.

"Watch, stand fast in the faith, be brave, be strong. Let all that you do be done with love." 1 Corinthians 16:13-14

Love changes everything. A smile or nice comment to her would've been good but God knew exactly what would speak to her the loudest. Provision. Generosity. Something she had apparently never experienced and had secretly always desired. That's why it's so important to see people the way God sees them and love them the way He loves them. All we have to do is be willing to do what He says, when and how He says to do it. That's how we change the world, one person at a time.

Take a Little Trip to Sychar

We can talk all we want about the need for reconciliation, but until we start living it we'll never have it. We have to lay down bitterness, envy, jealousy, and all our differences and live out love. Jesus demonstrated this best. He knew all about reconciliation. It's what He came for.

"Therefore, if anyone is in Christ, the new creation has come: the old has gone, the new is here! All this is from God, who reconciled us to himself through Christ and gave us the ministry of reconciliation: that God was reconciling the world to himself in Christ, not counting people's sins against them. And he has committed to us the message of reconciliation." 2 Corinthians 5:18 NIV

So how can we do this reconciliation thing like Jesus? I've heard it said, "Nobody cares what you know until they know that you care." We can reach out in love to those who sound, look, or act different. Outside our norms of comfort, we'll find the grandest opportunities to love like Jesus. He said:

> *"What you've done to the least of these, you've done to Me."*
> Matthew 25:40

Jesus didn't ask us to do anything He wasn't willing to do Himself. He said, when we feed the hungry, take in a stranger, clothe the naked, and visit the prisoners, He is pleased. What we've done (or not done) to the least of these, we've done to Him.

In John 4:1-42, we read about a woman who had gone to a well in the heat of the day in Samaria. She carried much shame and guilt because of her lifestyle and failures. She was well aware of what people thought of her, so she came to the well strategically at a time when she could avoid the judgmental whispers of onlookers.

> *"He (Jesus) needed to go through Samaria. So he came to the city of Samaria which is called Sychar, near the plot of ground that Jacob gave to his son Joseph." (verse 4)*

Jesus will meet us at our point of need. He will go where we are. He knows what we need better than we do. On this particular day, He needed to go through Samaria. Just like He knew everything about the woman I bought groceries for that day, He knew who would be at Jacob's well, and He knew exactly what she needed. He came to a city of Samaria, which is called Sychar. Jesus knew, before choosing His route for His journey, that this woman in Sychar was well worth Him going out of His way. According to Jewish law and tradition, He shouldn't have even been speaking to this woman.

She says in verse 9, *"How is it that you, being a Jew, ask a drink from me, a Samaritan woman? For Jews have no dealings with Samaritans."* Culturally, Jews and Samaritans hated one another. This hatred went all the way back to the days of Israel's kings. Israel's history included a civil war that had left them with 600 years of bitter hatred toward one another.

This woman had gone through five husbands and was currently living with a man. Five husbands? What could have possibly gone wrong five times? Jesus could have easily condemned her. Instead He pointed it out to show her He knew her and loved her unconditionally. This is what changed her. It's the kindness of the Lord that leads to repentance (Romans 2:4).

God sees past our past and into our future. He knows our frame and our purpose.

She had been pulling up water from an earthly well that ultimately never satisfied. No earthly relationship/man could fill the deepest longings of her heart. Jesus was willing to pour life into her thirsty soul. He offered a new source, a new start, and a new reputation.

Sychar in Greek means "purchased." Her redemption had been bought at a price. Jesus came to the Sychar of our lives to purchase our sin debts. It was costly, but He did it anyway. Are we willing to do the same thing, to go out of our way to love others even with our differences? We don't always have to agree, but we can still love.

Can't We Just Be Friends?

The church has long been divided. The word denomination comes from the same root word as denominator. The common denominator in math is referred to in division. For years we've been divided over everything except the One thing, Jesus. Now it's time we lay down everything that divides us and let the One thing that unites us be the main thing. Jesus came to reconcile and unify us. This was one of His main objectives in humbling Himself to walk this sod, and no doubt He wants his body reconciled to its members.

At a minimum, love is mandatory for this body to function properly. Pastor Farrell Lemings once said, "If we could get this love thing right, church would work." Not only is that true, but also, the body would thrive.

God's plan is for unity.

> *"Behold, how good and pleasant it is for brethren to dwell together in unity! It is like the precious oil upon the head, running down on the beard, the beard and of Aaron, running down on the edge of his garments. It is like the dew of Hermon, descending upon the mountains of Zion; for there the Lord commanded the blessing–Life forever forevermore." Psalm 133:1-3*

God is pleased when we can work together without fighting and complaining. It's like precious oil. Oil in the Bible is usually symbolic of the Spirit of God. So when we come together unified, the oil of the Spirit is poured out. When the Word of God, "the lamp" (Psalm 119:105), and the Holy Spirit, "the anointing oil" (Isaiah 61:1) collide, there's witness or testimony of the glory of God. Fire erupts in the presence. It's there in the place of unity and love that God commands a blessing, life forevermore.

Jesus Christ is the head of the Body. Imagine what it would be like to have a body with parts scattered all over the room. It be rather difficult to function properly, wouldn't it?

Division is the enemy's game. A kingdom divided against itself cannot stand, but we get to have the final word. We get to represent our Father's heart by humbling ourselves and coming together as one.

Jesus prayed: "I do not pray for these alone, but also for those who will believe in Me through their word; that they all may be one as You our Father, are in Me, and I in You; that they also may be one in Us, that the world may believe that You sent Me. And the glory which You gave Me I have given them, That they may be one just as We are one; I in them, and you in Me; that they may be made perfect in one, And that the world may know that You have sent Me, and have loved them as you have loved me." John 17:20-23

What a beautiful picture of family and unity. We are called to be family with Him and with one another...*that they may be one just as We are one.*

We can't continue down this path of disunity. It's as if we're in the dressing room, waiting in the Bridal chamber, readying ourselves for the coming of the Groom. In the meantime, our dress is torn with prejudice and denominationalism. Guess what. There aren't going to be denominations in heaven. We will all be worshiping as one big happy family.

The world is waiting for a strong church, full of life, to rise up and come to its aid. Meanwhile many are preoccupied with doctrinal disputes, walls of tradition and whether the worship experience is a style that suits us. How can a dismembered, unhealthy Body bring life and healing to a confused and dying world?

"Beloved, let us love one another, for love is of God; and everyone who loves is born of God and knows God. He who does not love does not know God, For God is love... beloved, if God so loved us, we also ought to love one another." 1 John 4:7-8, 11

43

A shift is coming. The sleeping giant of the church is slowly beginning to awaken and arise. She's waking up to who she is and what she has been destined to do. She's not going to settle for being dismembered. Many of the current issues that are dividing people are soon going to be swept away in the awesome move of God as we choose to love no matter what.

What Color is Love Anyway?

We have about 25,000 genes that make up the blueprint of the human body. Only two of these genes determine color. This means we are divided by .008 percent. Less than one percent of our genetic code determines the differences in our color. We are all basically the same. Yet, many people allow two little genes out of thousands to cause such hatred and division that it even costs people their lives.

Bishop E.W. Jackson, spoke at the North Carolina Renewal Project, a gathering of pastors from across the state. He said he was convinced, "If God wiped his hands across the earth and gave every human the same color skin and same texture hair but left some with green eyes, some with blue eyes, and some with brown eyes, it wouldn't be long till the green-eyed people would be in their corner. They'd be saying, 'Did you see how those people with brown eyes were looking at us?' Before you know it, they'd be forming an organization for the advancement of green-eyed people." He said, "The problem isn't the color of the skin, it's the sin."

I ask God lots of questions. During recent riots, I cried out to Him for answers and solutions, I felt His heart for America and I began weeping. He loves this country and the people here. He wants the very best for us, but largely we have turned our backs on Him.

We have a real dilemma. These outbursts are not the real problem;

they are symptoms of a deeper issue. Though we want to make this all about color, the real problem is a heart issue. We don't know how to love, because we don't know Love. There's so much hurt, bitterness, rejection, anger and fear. People are hopeless and responding from a place of brokenness. This doesn't condone irrational behavior, but it does explain it.

We all come from different backgrounds. I don't know what it's like to have never known my earthly father. Maybe you do. You may not understand the pain of walking through infertility. I do. We see through the lens of our own experience, which makes it difficult to understand others.

We all have a story. On this we can agree. We all have a choice to make, too. All our choices have consequences. At the end of our days, we'll look back and our lives will be made up of the sum of these choices. Will we allow the things done to us define our actions? Will we choose the higher road or will we choose to lower ourselves to our circumstances?

Quite honestly, my love for you has nothing to do with whether I understand you. It's all about my choosing to love you. Love in its purest and most basic form is love that has chosen to do so.

Did you know love doesn't have a color? Love doesn't see in color. Love doesn't even see in black and white. The color of love is having the ability to see people the way God sees them. Too many of us don't understand how He sees. The fact is, none of us deserve to be seen and loved the way Jesus loves. He's really the answer. HE IS LOVE. He is the Color of Love.

We need to release the Color of Love on every level in this country: all races, generations, denominations, male and female, sons to their fathers and fathers to their sons, and mothers and daughters. We are the generation God has chosen to restore the brokenness of the past. We have to realize we're in the battle of our lives.

> *"For we wrestle not against flesh and blood, but against principalities, against powers, against the rulers of the darkness of this world, against spiritual wickedness in high places." Ephesians 6:12*

We can fight and win! But we have to pray and choose, above all, to love.

> *"Clothe yourselves with compassion, kindness, humility, gentleness and patience. Bear with each other and forgive one another...And over all these virtues put on love, which binds them all together in perfect unity." Colossians 3:12-14*

It's time we rise up and speak up in love as the church. We have become far too silent. What are we afraid of?

> *"There is no fear in love, but perfect love casts out fear, because fear involves torment...we love him because he first loved us." 1 John 4:18-19*

Fear in this verse in Greek means "fobos," or flight. There is no fear in love. There is no "fobos" in love, meaning there's no flight in love. Love does not take flight. Love does not leave. Love stays. Love works out differences. God is love, and He's not leaving us. He will never leave us or forsake us. He's with us for the long haul. If God is for us, who can be against us? We can trust Him to love through us, to be what and who we can't be without Him.

We can't manufacture love on our own. It's not until we know perfect Love and learn to receive Him that we learn to love correctly. When His love saturates us, fills us to overflowing, then we love, because He loves through us. Tap into the Source of love, the One who gives us the ability to love. We may be inspired by a great message or by a person's enthusiasm for the Lord, but we are more likely to be changed when we have felt loved. We may not remember what was said but we WILL ALWAYS remember the value that was placed on us. *"In this the love of God was manifested toward us, that God has sent his only begotten son into the world, that we might live through him." 1 John 4:9* The enemy may try to steal, kill and destroy. He may try to cause all kinds of chaos and division, but Love wins. He already has!

Prayer:
Father, thank you for sending Jesus to save, heal and deliver us. Help us to see others through your eyes. Give us eyes tinted with the color of love, filtered by your grace. Holy Spirit move through us to bring reconciliation and restoration on the earth in our spheres of influence. In Jesus' name. Amen!

CHAPTER FOUR

Rise And Shine

"Once upon a breezy, glistening sea so fair, Love held His beloved whispering secrets there. He declared truth of her beauty and His unending love. No one had spoken such things to her. Her heart was undone."
~ Rivera Douthit {Ponderings}

OH HOW I'VE MISSED my loves as I'm away writing. My life is so richly blessed because of them. It's beautifully enchanting though, to spend time with my Love. His face enamors me. Morning by morning I awaken to be with Him, to hear Him, to learn from Him, to gaze upon Him...Jesus. His eyes of fire search me out, and I'm consumed by His love. The mystery of His relentless pursuit of His beloved, you and me, fascinates me. He never gives up. We're never too far-gone. His love reaches the far corners of the earth and back to find us.

Sally met Jesus and was saved at a young age, but all her life she was led to believe the lie that she was a burden and a mistake. Her mother's words were not affirming. She married a man who continuously cheated on her. Rejected at every turn, she was never enough, or at least she thought.

She stayed with her husband, and his promiscuity lead her to having unwanted health issues. To get back at him and in a desperate attempt to feel loved, she had an affair with her ex-boyfriend. The father of her first child was not her husband's. Her long kept secret separated her from God, who in her mind would never forgive her.

Sally had believed a lie about the nature of God. He is merciful and forgiving if we come to Him, turn away from our sin, and ask for forgiveness.

> *"If we confess our sins, He is faithful and just to forgive us our sins and to cleanse us from all unrighteousness." 1 John 1:9*

After a near death experience having her second daughter (who did belong to her husband), a woman from church gave Sally a profoundly impactful word from the Lord. In the two-page letter from God, there were two short yet life-changing lines.

"Daughter, you have been caught up in heavenly places with me to explore the depths of my love for thee. It is my desire to be with you, to share my love and bestow gifts."

Sally held onto those words through the ups and downs of the next thirty years. But trying to fill emptiness and numb her pain, she turned to drugs and became driven by personal goals, money and ambition.

> *"Why spend money on what is not bread, and your labor on*

what does not satisfy? Listen, listen to me, and eat what is good, and you will delight in the richest of fare." Isaiah 55:2

Looking back on that time, she wrote, "Satan has many ways of destroying lives. My choice was to use drugs as a painkiller. The problem with drugs as painkillers is that they work...for a while. This is the big lie. However, I bought the lie as when I was young, and this destructive pattern fit the bill. Years later I knew God had saved my life, my mind and my sanity. He delivered me. Plain and simple. God is in the saving business. He doesn't need anyone or anything. When God proclaims addiction out of your life, it ends."

One night about ten years ago, she had a God-dream, which she typically does not have. In this dream, Sally saw herself in a white wedding gown. Jesus was standing by a limousine opening the car door to have her get in to go to their wedding. Instead of getting in, she ran to the alley and climbed into a dumpster. She told Jesus she couldn't get in.

She wrote, "I woke up sobbing. He had shown me my shame. I still did not get it in its entirety. He had entered the private, secret sector of my heart and exposed it to the light. I became increasingly more miserable. I had this fire in me burning and nowhere to say it or breathe it."

"Therefore I am now going to allure her; I will lead her into the desert and speak tenderly to her." Hosea 2:14

God had been speaking through her entire life, beckoning her to come closer. Fearful and rebellious, she would run back to Egypt, to what was uncomfortably familiar—shame and rejection.

In the past couple of years, Sally and her new husband moved to

North Carolina. We met in a class I was teaching on my book, "Intimacy." Toward the last few days of class, Carole Ann was leading worship. God nudged me to go around the room and pray over individuals as He led. I would lay my hand gently on their shoulder and wait to hear from Him. I wanted to be led by the Holy Spirit in how to pray. To my surprise, He gave me a picture or word for each and every person I prayed over.

When I came to Sally, I waited. I was completely unaware that God had given her a dream just the night before. In the dream, she was in a white wedding dress, marrying Jesus, and He said, "You have been caught up in heavenly places with me to explore the depths of my love for thee." This was the same word He had given her through the woman at church thirty years before. The theme of the dream was a continuation of the dream she had with Jesus and the limousine ten years before.

That same night her earthly husband, who was in bed beside her, woke up. He found her weeping beside their bed. He said, "Honey, what is going on? Jesus just came to me in a dream and told me you had married Him." She told her husband about the dream she just had of marrying Jesus, and they both began to cry. God had come to them at the same time with the same message. This was one of the most pivotal, life-changing moments for her with God and her husband.

The next day in our class, I laid my hand on her shoulder as I waited to hear from God. He let me see her in a white wedding gown. I leaned down close to her ear and said, "God showed me a picture of you in a white wedding gown. I believe He wants you to know you belong to Him. You are His Bride, and He loves you." She wept uncontrollably. She could hardly talk clearly enough to tell me why she was crying. Undone. Elated. Tears of joy flowed. Since that night and morning, she's never been the same.

> *"There I will give her back her vineyards, and will make the Valley of Achor a door of hope. There she will respond as in the days of her youth, as in the day she came up out of Egypt. "In that day," declares the Lord, "you will call me 'my husband'; you will no longer call me 'my master.'" Hosea 2:15-16*

When her daughter became an adult, Sally finally told her the truth. One of the very things she had feared the most came to pass. Again rejection. Her daughter felt betrayed as though her entire life had been a lie. Sally's relationship with her daughter has been strained, leaving her feeling wounded and lonely. This time, she's not shaken. No. She's resting. She trusts. She believes. Sally has a knowing as she's held by Love that He will restore. He will give her back her vineyards, and in the valley make a door of hope.

> *"I will betroth you to me forever; yes, I will betroth you to me in righteousness and justice, In lovingkindness And mercy; I will betroth you to me in faithfulness, and you shall know the Lord." Hosea 2:19-20*

God had Hosea pen those words over two thousand years ago, and they still remain. Hosea means "deliverer." Gomer, his beloved, means "complete." God told Hosea to marry a harlot, so he married Gomer and had a son with her. The book of Hosea is a type, meaning it is a character or story symbolizing God with Israel and Christ with His Bride.

Tarnished by shame and sin, many of us keep running from the very One who will free us. We try to fill our emptiness with money, people, and things that don't satisfy. Our behavior is a result of what we think of ourselves. How we view ourselves is directly related to how we view

God and whether we trust Him. He's saying, *"Don't call me Master. Call me Husband. I will restore you completely. I will deliver you."*

When we look at ourselves and see undeserving, God sees one set apart for His delight, one who is good enough and worthy of love. We don't deserve anything He's done for us, yet we're recipients of His riches. There's a fine line between deserving nothing yet having rights to everything, simply because we're His. We're not mistresses, we are His Bride, made pure, holy and without blemish. Open your eyes. Look into His and see your reflection there. You captivate him.

> *"I'm my lover's. I'm all He wants. I'm all the world to Him."*
> *Song of Solomon 7:11 (MSG)*

Oh Jesus, we're so in love with you.

> *"No longer will they call you Deserted, or name your land Desolate. But you will be called Hephzibah, and your land Beulah; for the LORD will take delight in you, and your land will be married."*
> *Isaiah 62:4*

Awake Awake

I recall a flight from California to North Carolina when I slept the entire trip. Before we landed, the flight attendant so sweetly nudged me and said, "Rise and shine mornin' glory. It's time to get up." Clearly she was from the South. I heard similar words as a child growing up in North Carolina. Having lived in California for a few years at that point, the sound of her southern accent was so endearing and comforting to my homesick heart. Her words made it easy, actually rather exciting, to wake up and face the day. I knew it wouldn't be long until I'd be home.

Home is such a special place. They say it's where our heart is. If that's the case, my home is strewn all over, because my heart is in many different places with those I love. Home is a place of comfort, family, inheritance and belonging. It's where we can let our hair down and be ourselves without fear of rejection. This is what we find with our Father. Home.

According to Isaiah 54, when we make our home with our Father, the following rightfully belong to us:

- ➢ Sing (songs).
- ➢ Increase (enlarge) your territory.
- ➢ You won't be ashamed or remember the shame of your youth (your past)
- ➢ The Lord has called you.
- ➢ He is your Husband.
- ➢ He's not angry with you.
- ➢ He has made a covenant (promise) with you, like with Noah.
- ➢ Your house will be rebuilt and laid with colorful gems.
- ➢ You shall be established in righteousness.
- ➢ You shall not be afraid (no fear).
- ➢ No weapon formed against you will prosper.
- ➢ Every tongue that rises against you or judges you, you shall refute (condemn).

This is our inheritance! THIS!

Jesus also has an inheritance as the Son. His greatest inheritance is us. It's intimacy with His beautiful Bride.

Too many of us feel the need to work to earn God's love and acceptance. Yes we should do things for Him but only as an overflow of our love for Him, not to manipulate Him into loving us more. We do for Him out *of* love, not *for* love. Intimacy with God, truly knowing Him is ours. All we have to do is lean in and receive it. I've heard it said that religion indicates we have to earn something, and intimacy teaches us to receive. This means we have His love perfectly without ever doing a thing. We can rest in Him. Rest in His love for us. Rest in genuine relationship. He demonstrated His love on the cross before we were born. We don't have to work for it. We don't have to strive for His acceptance. We are not lost or invisible to Him. He sees us. He notices us. We have an inheritance and He loves us fully, simply because we're His.

The world is filled with broken people in need of this truth. Remember how the prodigal son had to be reminded of who he was and what would be waiting for him at home? He had gone away, spent his inheritance, and found himself eating with pigs. At the lowest point of his life and completely stripped of pride, he decided he would go home and work for his father as a servant. His father saw him coming down the road to their house, and he ran to his son with arms open wide. He was ecstatic to see him, to have him home and to know he was alive. It mattered not to the father where his son had been or how long he'd been gone. He threw a big party to celebrate and welcome him home. The father even put his signet ring on his son and seated him in a position of honor and authority over all that he owned. Why? Because of love. Because the one who had been lost had now been found.

This is what Love does. This is what God does when He sees us coming. He runs to us. We belong to him. People need to know they are loved, and they are welcome to come back home. They need to know where they belong. Too many don't even know yet that they are His. They need healing, light, and life. We are called to be the light and shine in the dark places of the earth.

"Arise, shine, for your light has come, and the glory of the Lord rises upon you. See, darkness covers the earth and thick darkness is over the peoples, but the Lord rises upon you and his glory appears over you." Isaiah 60:1-2

People need someone like you or me to come along and represent Jesus to them. He needs us, the church, to step up and illuminate the darkness in their weary, dried-up souls. They need to know their Father's unending love.

Breathe

About a year ago, I had a dream I was on a dark freeway. There had been a wreck with multiple cars involved. People were lying all over the road and on the sides. A crowd had gathered to try to help. As I came on the scene, I noticed the people on the ground had no scratches or apparent injuries, but they all looked dead. They were unresponsive. We tried to call 911 when someone spoke up and said, "Oh yeah, they changed their hours. The emergency response is not available after a certain time."

There was an urgency but no availability to emergency responders, and people appeared dead. There's a similar unresponsive complacency in the church today. Unavailable in many ways, we have been asleep to a world dead and in need of us.

We've often heard it said that hurting people hurt people. Each time we turn on the news, we see it. Rioting, hatred, bitterness, and violence appear at every turn. This is what the Bible calls lawlessness.

"Everyone who sins breaks the law; in fact, sin is lawlessness." 1 John 3:4

57

"It is shameful even to mention what the disobedient do in secret. But everything exposed by the light becomes visible—and everything that is illuminated becomes a light. This is why it is said: "Wake up, sleeper, rise from the dead, and Christ will shine on you." Ephesians 5:12-14 (NIV)

Oh, that the Bride of Christ would awaken from her sleep to arise and shine to live the fullest life.

The Holy Spirit brought Ezekiel into a valley. What His eyes beheld there was probably horrifying, a valley filled with dead people. Bones were everywhere and they were very dry, meaning these people had been dead awhile. In the natural, God was showing Ezekiel the spiritual state of His beloved Israel. God spoke to Ezekiel and said:

"Prophesy to these bones and say to them, 'Dry bones, hear the word of the Lord! This is what the Sovereign Lord says to these bones: I will make breath enter you, and you will come to life. I will attach tendons to you and make flesh come upon you and cover you with skin; I will put breath in you, and you will come to life. Then you will know that I am the Lord.'"

So Ezekiel prophesied. He spoke to the bones and they *"came together, bone to bone."*

Then God said, "Prophesy to the breath...and say to it, 'This is what the Sovereign Lord says: Come, breath, from the four winds and breathe into these slain, that they may live.'"

Ezekiel prophesied, *"and breath entered them; they came to life and stood up on their feet—a vast army."* Then God told Ezekiel these dry bones represented Israel, and by His Spirit they too would live. *(Ezekiel 37:1-14)*

People are broken and injured in spirit. God needs bold, obedient ones like Ezekiel who are willing to prophesy to the dry bones in people's lives. He's calling us up and out to be His hands, feet and mouthpiece. We need Him. We need one another. A dead man can't help anyone. The living are the ones who call for help, or intervene to help others.

> *"By his power God raised the Lord from the dead, and he will raise us also." 1 Corinthians 6:14*

Seeds die before they go into the earth and burst back through. New life is springing up. The winter is gone. Spring has come. Alive, we are entering into a new season.

> *"Who is this coming up from the wilderness, Leaning upon her beloved? I awakened you under the apple tree. There your mother brought you forth; There she who bore you brought you forth. Set me as a seal upon your heart, As a seal upon your arm; For love is as strong as death, Jealousy as cruel as the grave; Its flames are flames of fire, A most vehement flame." Song of Solomon 8:5-6*

Pastor Byron Wicker says, "Death takes everything. Death demands all. Love is as strong as death, but it gives all." The Spirit of God inside us won't settle for us being wounded, bound up, imprisoned, and spiritually emaciated. He is love, and His goal is always to set us free to soar. We know He is the only One capable of doing it.

We've all had wilderness seasons when we've felt alone, sick, confused, and down. The wilderness can be a place of great desolation and temptation. Satan whispers lies in our weakness. He would love to convince us that we're not good enough, invisible or a failure. Remember Jesus was in the wilderness for forty days. He was tempted by Satan in that place but never sinned. He came through to the other side of His wilderness period full of power and His

59

earthly ministry followed. If we choose to rest on Jesus and the truth in those difficult seasons, we will come through the wilderness refined and ready to do more than we ever imagined.

We can choose to respond to what we know rather than what we feel. Feelings and truth do not always align. I choose to believe God even when I can't see Him. Truth doesn't change when our emotions do. God doesn't change either. Because we can't feel, hear, or see Him clearly doesn't mean He's not there. Who is this coming out of the wilderness leaning on her beloved? Rest. Still yourself in His presence, even when it seems that everything around you is falling apart. Awaken to His heart to carry you when you can't carry yourself. We're breathed on by God. The breath of His Spirit, like the fragrance of apples under the apple tree, awakens us with His love.

> *"Awake and sing, you who dwell in dust; For your dew is like the dew of herbs, And the earth shall cast out the dead." Isaiah 26:19b*

We are not in slavery; we're in love. When we believe in Jesus (and what He did on the cross for us), we're saved. When we realize He believes in us, we're changed. It's true. He believes in us so much He died for us. When we truly get this, we're marked by it forever.

He gazes upon us with total confidence and love. He looks us in the eyes and says, "Rise and shine morning glory. Time to get up. We've got important things to do together." The sound of His voice speaking those words makes it easy, actually rather exciting, to wake up and face the day.

> *"My beloved spoke and said to me, 'Arise, my darling, my beautiful one, come with me. See! The winter is past; the rains are over and gone. Flowers appear on the earth; the season of*

singing has come, the cooing of doves is heard in our land. The fig tree forms its early fruit; the blossoming vines spread their fragrance. Arise, come, my darling; my beautiful one, come with me.'" Song of Songs 2:10-14 (NIV)

At my seaside writing retreat, the ocean dazzles in sunlight, and something in me is awakened. Water dances with life and light in worship of its Creator. This is what happens in His presence. We come alive. We sparkle. We dance, for the One and Only has breathed life, far beyond ordinary life. It's extravagant. It's a forever life that lifts us out of pits and problems to set our souls and soles on His rock, high above all that hinders. In Him, we live and move and have our being and nothing else matters.

We've been chosen and called to arise into our places of destiny. Jesus is whispering, "Arise. Come away with me my beloved. Oh the stories I have to tell you, and the adventures we will have together. I will cause you to shine." Aware of our rich inheritance, we realize who we are. Awakened. We are His beautiful Bride standing tall, a force to be reckoned with—free and home at last.

Prayer:
Jesus, Awaken your Bride to her healing, forgiveness, salvation and deliverance. Call her into her true identity and use us to ready the Bride for your coming! Help us to receive your forgiveness and redemption in our own lives, so we can confidently step out of shame and live in confidence to be who you created us to be. Give us courage to speak to the valley of dry bones in our own lives and prophesy over those dry bones to arise and live. In Jesus' name. Amen!

CHAPTER FIVE

Loose The Fetters

*"Let Thy goodness, like a fetter,
bind my wandering heart to Thee."*
~ Robert Robinson

THE WORDS WOKE ME as they repeated in my spirit, "Loose the fetters... loose the fetters...loose the fetters." I knew it could've only been from God because I wasn't even sure if I had ever heard the term "fetter." I had to look it up. In Merriam-Webster's Dictionary, a fetter is "a chain/shackle for the feet, or something that confines."

It's used in Isaiah 58:6, *"Is this not that fast I have chosen: To loose the bonds of wickedness (fetters), undo the heavy burdens, let the oppressed go free, and that you break every yoke?"*

God's heart is that we would be loosed from all chains of wickedness, whatever they might be. "Let the oppressed go free." Notice He didn't say, "I'm going to let the oppressed go free." He indicates here that He has appointed US to loose the fetters and set the oppressed free. It's our job to co-labor with God in this. We have been given the authority to do so. How we do this may vary. It could be creating a worldwide campaign to end the sex slave industry, or it could be simply listening to someone's story and speaking truth over the lies they've long believed. Either way, God is calling us to rise up and break the bonds of wickedness.

Jesus was so good at this! As a matter of fact, He walked the earth to show us how to do it. I've always loved the story of the woman who had been crippled for eighteen years. Luke 13 says Satan bound her with a spirit causing her sickness. Jesus spoke, *"Woman you are loosed [from the spirit that binds you] from your infirmity" (verse 12)*. Then he touched her and she stood up straight. Transformed in an instant, her mind was free of unbelief and hopelessness. No longer would she be an outcast. She arose into a new dimension of Jesus' love for her. She had experienced His love and healing firsthand, rather than standing on the sidelines just hearing about it.

So many people have gotten stuck bent over in life by the lies they've believed. They assume they can't be healed. They think God can heal, but He wouldn't do it for them. They never ask because they don't want to be a bother. Some people feel unworthy to be free, because of their sin and the condemnation they've felt as a result. Shame has overtaken their thinking. The list goes on. All lies. There's nothing more satisfying than speaking the absolute truth over a long believed lie. I've heard it said that evangelism in its purest form is telling someone they are enough. Evangelism is not just telling people about Jesus, it's showing them Jesus. When we show them Jesus' love, we show them they are enough.

Loosed

Two years ago while with a group of women in Moravian Falls, North Carolina, I made a simple statement and a gasp carried through the room. I said, "Intimacy requires trust. Some of us can't be intimate with God because we don't trust Him. Why do you suppose we don't trust?" What concerned them was what surfaced in their hearts as a result of the question. Why do you suppose we don't trust Him? A simple question resurrected all kinds of answers and unwanted feelings. Issues of the heart: trauma, brokenness, shame, regret, loneliness, rejection, and years of feeling invisible. Many unwanted emotions raised their ugly heads in that moment and tears flowed freely.

One woman, shyly asked, "Why did He let it happen?" The Holy Spirit gave me discernment to know she had probably been sexually abused. She wasn't alone. The enemy wanted her to think she was alone, but she wasn't. That's probably the number one question people have. "Why, Lord? Why did You let this happen? Why didn't you stop it?" People who have been victimized by abuse or lost someone close unexpectedly often ask why. With one look at the injustice in the world, it doesn't take long for us to ask why.

Remember in the Garden of Eden when sin entered the world? That's why sick, broken people are taking matters into their own hands operating in the kingdom of darkness. This gives us even more of a reason to arise into our places as the Body of Christ. We are called to be salt and light, world shifters for the kingdom of God. Before the fall of man, in the world the way God originally designed it, those horrible things wouldn't have happened. But, because of evil, rebellion and free will, lots of terrible things happen. God will have His justice for all the wickedness in this world when Jesus returns.

Toward the end of our time together at the retreat, we were praying, sharing and getting ready to say our goodbyes. The questioning woman spoke up and began sharing her story. Her words spewed out like poison being released from a festering wound. As the pressure of all that had been bottled up inside her for a lifetime was released, God began the process of healing. She had been a victim of sexual abuse and incest. She became pregnant at a young age and was forced to have an abortion. Every day shame had held her in bondage to the lie that she was not good enough. She felt dirty and like it was all her fault. As a result she's never been married or had children.

Remember what happened when Lazarus died? Jesus didn't come for four days. Lazarus' body was already decaying. His sister, Martha, questioned Jesus in John 11, *"Lord, if You had been here, my brother would not have died" (verse 21).* This was a statement of faith as well as an accusation. We often say we believe in God. We know with our minds He has all power to heal, deliver, save, and resurrect, but do we really believe it? When something goes wrong, we want to blame Him and wonder why He didn't come immediately to our rescue.

Let's get this straight. God doesn't will bad things to happen to us. It is always His desire for our good. He may reprimand and discipline us at times, as any good father does for his children, but He always does it in a loving way. Regardless of our choices (or the things chosen for us), God's goodness never changes. He's good when we are not. He's good when others are not. His nature is good. His thoughts toward us are lovely and true. He wants us healed and living in freedom. We're His children. Just as most people want the very best for their children, so does God (even more so, because His love for us is perfect).

The timing of His rescue is often so others can benefit. Freedom of the one brings deliverance of many, *"...that they might believe" (verse 42).*

Jesus thanked God before the miracle, then He said, "Lazarus, come forth." This was as simple for Jesus as waking someone who had been sleeping. The Word says, "He who had died came out bound hand and foot with grave clothes." He had been awakened to Jesus, yet He was still bound. This was also the case with our friend. She knew Jesus. She could even hear His voice. But she was still bound by the shame and scars of her past. Just because we have said a prayer of salvation doesn't mean we've been delivered from all our bondages and set free from our past.

Then Jesus said to them, *"Loose him and let him go."* Free him! Get Lazarus out of those grave clothes, so he can arise and run free. Release my beloved friend out of all that is binding him and holding him back. He's saying that to many of us today!

Oh the heartbreak every woman in that room experienced with her. What we witnessed that day was much the same as what they witnessed at the tomb of Lazarus. Though none of us had walked in her shoes, we felt her pain. We loved her. We touched her, hugged her, and prayed for her. She asked God for forgiveness. We prayed deliverance from all the lying, tormenting spirits that had for years kept her bound. We invited the Holy Spirit to saturate her entire being: body, mind, soul, and spirit.

"Loose" in the story of Lazarus is from the Greek word *"lyo,"* meaning to loosen a person or thing tied or fastened. The word, lyo, refers to tied feet, or a husband and wife bound in marriage. To loose one bound. To undo or dissolve a legal agreement. To do away with, to deprive of authority. It refers to freeing of bondage, and indicates a legal binding being reversed.

Because of what Jesus did on the cross, Satan no longer has any legal authority over God's children. What he's tried to do in the past, to tie us up and prevent us from living our God-given potential, has been reversed on the cross. Jesus gets the final word. The cross has given Jesus the keys to annul any legal rights Satan may have thought he had to us. That's why when Jesus reveals Himself everything

67

changes. He defeated death and took back the keys to God's kingdom and everything that rightfully belongs to us. We were never made to be in covenant with the enemy.

Without realizing it we can be tied to all kinds of things—from past/present relationships to places and things. This is normal, and there are good and bad ties. This happens when we allow our mind, will, and emotions to become connected to the person, place, thing, or idea. Unhealthy ties need to be loosed or cut. For example, if you have experienced recurring manipulation, control, or a belittling spirit within a relationship, this is unhealthy. I'm not referring to a spat in a marriage or a little disagreement in a friendship. There is a big difference. I'm talking about being loosed from a bond of wickedness. Prayer and fasting give us wisdom, strength and strategy to be able to break these bonds (fetters). It can seem difficult because of compassion for the person, love for an item, place, or even a certain way of thinking. To move forward with the Lord and remain in a healthy place spiritually the loosing must be done.

> *"Assuredly, I say to you, whatever you bind on earth will be bound in heaven, and whatever you loose on earth will be loosed in heaven. Again I say to you that if two of you agree on earth concerning anything that they ask, it will be done for them by My Father in heaven. For where two or three are gathered together in My name, I am there in the midst of them." Matthew 18:18-20*

A simple prayer will do to begin the process of loosing the unhealthy ties. I emphatically suggest praying in agreement with one to two like-minded, trustworthy believers. The prayer for cutting off unhealthy ties (also known as deliverance) might go something like this:

"In the name of Jesus I loose myself from manipulation, addiction, sexual sin, pornography, homosexuality, depression, oppression, rejection, abandonment, abuse, control, gluttony, and _____. I bind these and cast them off, away from me. I cut off soul and fleshly ties I've had with (name of the people ___, which may include people from the past with whom we've had emotional, physical, or spiritual ties). Father, I thank You for releasing me and setting me free from these. I ask for and receive Your forgiveness and healing. I ask you to pour your Spirit into every place that is now vacant within me, in Jesus' name. Fill me up, Holy Spirit!"

By Jesus' stripes we are healed (Isaiah 53:5). I've heard it said that stripes means "fellowship." By His fellowship, we are healed. When we're in personal fellowship with Jesus, healing, deliverance, and resurrection are going to happen. Life. He gives life!

Jesus had entered the room with us that day in the mountains. The life of the Spirit of God began to flood the place. He saturated the crevices of her weary, broken heart. As His life and peace were released, this daughter of the King stood upright with her head held high. She walked out on the front porch of this quaint mountain lodge, and with a voice strong and mighty, she yelled, "YES! YES! YES LORD!!! FREEDOM!" The sound of heaven roared and echoed through those hills. We sat inside listening as she yelled outside. There wasn't a dry eye in the room. We witnessed emotional, spiritual, and physical transformation. The weight she once carried had been lifted. Her gait was straighter and countenance brighter. She was free!

> *"I will lift up my eyes to the hills—from whence comes my help? My help comes from the Lord, Who made heaven and earth. He will not allow your foot to be moved; He who keeps you will not slumber." Psalm 121:1-3*

Our Stories

Confession is so powerful! There's a courage and authenticity that is required to share our stories. Releasing our hidden secrets scatters the darkness and makes room for the healing light of love, belonging, worthiness, and joy to shine in. We have to be okay with being seen, naked, and vulnerable.

> *"Therefore confess your sins to each other and pray for each other so that you may be healed. The prayer of a righteous person is powerful and effective." James 5:16 (NIV)*

Much like the broken shells on the seashore, there's beauty and purpose in our brokenness. It never goes unnoticed or unused. Part of beauty of humanity is our imperfections. The sum of our lives is for us to be changed from glory to glory, while resting in Jesus' perfection and ability to make us more like Him.

Since that Moravian Falls retreat there have been several women with stories almost identical to the woman who roared FREEDOM that day. Truth is, we all have a story. We all have a past with some hurts and/or regret. We ALL need freedom from something: pride, judgment, perfectionism, materialism, wrong thinking, guilt, unforgiveness, lying, bitterness, etc. Some of us have brought our stories on ourselves, while others' stories were brought on them. Either way, God has chosen to forgive us and set us free. And so it goes, our stories are used for His glory. He has a way of recycling garbage into a fine work of art—that is what we are—beautifully designed, purposed works of art.

We can't help free anyone else if our own hands are tied. We have to be free ourselves to help set others free. When we allow Jesus to touch whatever needs to be transformed, everything else falls away and all we see is Grace. His love reaches the far corners of our hearts, disintegrating the pain of the past. With one word from Him demons have to flee. The shackles of shame break loose, freeing us from the prison of despair and the heaviness of guilt. Gone. Gone forever. And WE. ARE. FREE.

Prayer:
Jesus, thank you for coming to set the captives free. You don't leave us bound, but you loose us from our grave clothes. Thank you for freedom. Help us share with others to bring them into freedom as well. Enable us to loose the captives by the power of Your Spirit. In Jesus' name. Amen.

CHAPTER SIX

Hope Beyond Hope

*"There is no pit so deep that His love is
not deeper still."*
~ Corrie ten Boom

DURING A THREE-MONTH season of weekly teaching, I took women through the Word and my book, "Intimacy: into me You see." It was sweet to witness the light coming on spiritually for women. Revelation of God's love, and His desire for them in intimacy became tangible and life changing. So many were set free to soar.

This rewarding season was also one of my most challenging. About a month into teaching, I had a mammogram that was questionable. So, I returned the following week for a follow-up. While I was waiting and not knowing what was going on, the what-ifs began to creep in. Unrest and fear tried to grip my thoughts. After the follow-up, the radiologist decided he needed to do a biopsy. That led to another wait, another appointment, and more unexpected expense. Everything turned out okay in the end, but the process was tedious and stressful, to say the least. After the third mammogram, I was diagnosed with shingles on my torso on the same side. This was all within a period of about a month, and I assumed it was a result of the trauma my body had undergone.

Having shingles was the worst pain I had ever experienced. All I could do was choose to trust and lean in even closer to God. At times I felt like John, who leaned up against Jesus' chest. It was a beautifully intimate time with God, but I was miserable and it was humiliating to navigate through.

One of the things I sensed God wanted was for the women in class to learn to have hope and perseverance under trial. Week after week, I'd teach. God would ask me to be vulnerable to share my personal experiences. During this time, it was difficult to wear anything touching my skin. Pressing through, God healed me from shingles in roughly two weeks. Sometimes we press through and God doesn't send a miracle...sometimes He does, but it is longer before He sends it. In my case, I knew the quick healing was miraculous, and this group of women got to witness it. Perseverance through trial was demonstrated and the healing power of God was made manifest.

One day while the shingles were at their height of pain and intensity, the Lord told me to go to church with my best friend, Carole Ann. There was a visiting evangelist from India, who was known for His ability to hear the voice of the Lord. Without knowing anything about my current circumstances or me, he began praying for me, "Father thank you for this blessed child, stretch your mighty hand upon this...Oh woman of God. (pause) Something cut down some tree. Some attacks came and cut down the tree, but many buds are coming up. You (talking to me) have lost one, but multiple blessings are coming up in Jesus' name. Now multiple blessings. And the Lord is really acknowledging the territories. Like a water which is running through new roots, the Holy Spirit is going to take you to a new limb of life. New experiences. New spiritual experiences. New depth of God's word and height of His glory! These are going to be experienced in your life in the mighty name of Jesus."

This prophetic man heard correctly. Attacks came and cut down the tree of pride and self-will in my life. It may have been the enemy trying to destroy me, but God used it for my good and the good of others. As a result of being stripped, cut down and humbled, many new buds were coming up in its place. Life and multiplication were occurring. Hope and complete trust in God were being birthed out of difficult circumstances. I had to be yielded. The more broken I felt, the stronger He was making me. Ultimately, I was in a process of becoming more like Him.

> *"For there is hope for a tree, if it is cut down, that it will sprout again, and that its tender shoots will not cease. Though its root may grow old in the earth, and its stump may die in the ground, yet at the scent of water it will bud and bring forth branches like a plant." Job 14:7-9*

Recently I asked God what it meant when Paul said, "...that I may know Him [Jesus] and the power of His resurrection and the fellowship of His sufferings, being conformed to His death; *in order that I may attain to the resurrection from the dead." Philippians 3:10-11*

He answered, "Rivera, nothing can be resurrected that hasn't first died."

Death has to occur before resurrection can become a possibility. If there's been no death, there's no need for a resurrection. God has been teaching me on a deeper level the necessity of dying to myself: my abilities, desires, expectations, and even opinions.

Self has to be put to death daily, so He can bring forth His purposes and more of the character of Jesus can be made evident in us. If we're always aiming for the way we think things should be, we'll never experience fully what He intended them to be. We leave no room for God's will, if our focus is on our own demands and desires. He reminds me often of Jesus' prayer, "Thine is the kingdom, and the power, and the glory." Not "Mine is the kingdom." It's His kingdom, not ours. It's His power, not ours. It's His glory, not ours. I don't know about you, but I want Him seated on the throne in my life, not me. He's Lord, not me. He's in the lead position, making all the right decisions.

The necessity is for us to get low and realize who we are in relation to Him. This is true humility. There's a confidence in humility because it's realizing who we are on an even deeper level. In a generation of entitlement, there's a tension between realizing who we are as sons and daughters and realizing who we are not. We're not God. We deserve everything and nothing all at the same time. Everything is ours because we are His children, and nothing is ours apart from Jesus. Our heavenly Father didn't have to give what He gave, but He did.

The revelation of death and pruning for the new to be birthed gives hope when all seems hopeless. The "tree being cut down" can feel like there's no hope in sight. But God who is rich in mercy resurrects the dead, restores what's been lost, and mends things broken. God wants what's best for us, and sometimes that requires pruning. He's more concerned with our character than our calling. He's ultimately looking at our motives and the intent of our heart. He wants a purified, unblemished Bride, filled with the hope of her salvation and ready to step into her calling.

A heart without hope is shriveled, dry and dead and can give no life to the body. But, a heart with hope stays alive. Just as blood carries oxygen to the entire body, hope oxygenates our souls. At the scent of water that dead tree will bud and bring forth branches. Up and out of that fertile ground where hope has watered the seed of promise, the soul lives.

Press In and Press On

"Hope deferred makes the heart sick, but a longing fulfilled is a tree of life." Proverbs 13:12

Kayce and I met in the class I was teaching when I was diagnosed with shingles. Since I've known her, she's always been an upbeat, joyful, and a glass-half-full kind of person. She shared how God told her more than twenty years ago, while she was sitting in a church service, that she would one day have a ministry called Haven. He gave her a few details including the scripture that went with His word for her. For twenty-three years in hopeful expectation, Kayce believed God for the day she would finally open Haven. It was to be a place of rest and refueling in the (Holy) Spirit for members of Methodist clergy and their wives. Kayce's desire was that they would walk in and feel loved by God. Her entire 50 years of marriage had been devoted to ministry. Having been a Methodist pastor's wife, she personally knew the need for ministers to have a place of respite where they would feel valued. God knew He had created her for loving people through her gift of hospitality. God knew she was the perfect one for the job, so He birthed Haven in her heart.

After she shared with me a few years ago about her word from God, I prayed with her and have had the privilege of watching it unfold. Along the way, her vision of how she thought Haven would look has changed from time to time. It didn't turn out exactly as she thought, but it turned out even better. She thought it might be in a serene, mountain-like setting, but one of her favorite places to visit has always been the beach. As she continued praying into God's promise, she said it was uncanny how often she started seeing and receiving things with seashells.

At an event I was hosting at The Cove in the mountains of North Carolina, there were various gifts for the women. The woman who had prepared them wrapped every gift in its own unique packaging. God told her to wrap this huge conch shell in a brown paper bag. Sure enough, no one else picked it because it wasn't in a pretty package, so Kayce ended up with it. When she opened it, she cried. It was yet another confirmation from God that her Haven might be found at the beach.

Kayce had bid on a beach property. Exactly twenty-three years later to the day that God had spoken this word, she received a call that her bid had been accepted. Her dream was becoming a reality. If God says it, He means it. If it's already established in heaven, then calling it forth from heaven to earth through prayer and belief is our job.

> "May the God of all hope fill you with all joy and peace in believing [through the experience of your faith] that by the power of the Holy Spirit you will abound in hope an overflow with confidence in his promises." Romans 15:13

Hope leads to confidence, not of ourselves, but of His promises. He is the seed of promise. Everything He's promised He will do.

> "For when God made the promise to Abraham, since He could swear by no one greater, He swore by Himself, saying, 'I will surely bless you and i will surely multiply you.'" Hebrews 6:13-14 (NIV)

God stood in the courts of heaven and swore to Abraham by His own name. There's no greater name in heaven or earth. Abraham knew God, so he hoped without doubting. The world hopes by wishing for something. Supernatural hope is attached to a confidence in God and believes for the miraculous. This is the hope that knows who God is and of what He's capable. Faith filled hope—it knows no limits and believes the very best. We can trust that when God promises us something He will do it, because His promises are sworn on oath by His own name.

In Romans 4, we read that Abraham became that which was spoken, a father of many nations. He believed God and it was accounted to him as righteousness. Without faith we can't please God. Unbelief hinders us from seeing God, and the miracle.

> *"He did not waver at the promise of God through unbelief, but was strengthened in faith, giving glory to God, and being fully convinced that what He had promised He was also able to perform."*
> *Romans 4:20-21*

Abraham had hope that went beyond the natural. He didn't just wish for it, he knew it would be fulfilled because God had spoken it. His hope had vision for what would be.

Dream Big

When God asked me to write this book, He said He wanted me to go away for two weeks to write. I could definitely think of all the reasons this would probably not be possible. But, there was no good reason to refrain from asking Him for it. I laid my requests before Him for a hidden getaway in which to work, with Internet access, and help for my family while I was gone. Soon after praying, I had three different offers for quiet getaways to write.

"Beach Haven" became a little piece of heaven on earth while I wrote. My friend's long hoped for word of the Lord became a reality in a "faith-full," "hope-full" woman's life. As He's fulfilling promises for Kayce, He's allowed her dreams to intersect with mine.

We can't fulfill our destiny in our own strength, but we can yield ourselves to the destiny of God all the days of our lives. We can't produce the promises of God, but we can believe Him for them. We can say yes, trust God, and carry them in our hearts until they are birthed in Him. Nothing is impossible for those who believe. When we can dream with God-inspired vision and hope without doubting, we will leave a legacy. Our zeal will contagiously encourage others, and our stories will shape history. We get to come alongside what God is doing on the earth to be a part of His-story.

> He says, "I am the Lord, the God of all flesh, is anything too hard for me?" Jeremiah 32:27

Many of us have witnessed God part the Red Sea in our lives more than once. We've seen miracles, whether or not we've acknowledged them as such. He's often positioned us to do things we never thought were possible, until we were courageous enough to believe with Him. Two keys to seeing the birth of a promise: believing God and showing up. This book would never have been a possibility if I had not heard and trusted God with the idea and then showed up to do the work.

He will confirm His dreams to us. If He can hold the stars in place and remember them all by name, a little confirmation isn't too much for God. When He confirms and plants His ideas in us, He'll breathe life on them and help birth them at just the right time. Align your heart with what He's depositing in you. Let His dreams for you grow, and a beautifully surrendered life of worship and creativity will blossom forth.

Trust

During that season of teaching when I had shingles, as I was preparing to teach a week ahead of time, God said, "I want you to go unprepared."

I was still questioning if I'd heard right, when the morning arrived for me to teach. I stood up and scanned across the room. Of all days, the pastor of women's ministry had slipped in to listen on the morning I was to show up with no plan or preparation. I hesitantly said, "I'm the most unprepared today than I've ever been in my history of teaching." It grew uncomfortably silent and there was even a little gasp in the room. I continued, "The Lord asked me to come without a plan, completely unprepared. I had to be obedient. In being the most unprepared I've ever been I'm the most prepared. God is with me. I know He's all I need. He's my preparation." Another deep breath and the room lightened a little.

> *"Blessed is the man [or woman] who TRUSTS in the Lord, And whose HOPE is the Lord. For he shall be like a tree planted by the waters, which spreads out its roots by the river, and WILL NOT FEAR when heat comes; But its leaf will be green, And will NOT BE ANXIOUS in the year of drought, nor will cease from yielding fruit." Jeremiah 17:7-8*

God was teaching us trust. He was showing all of us just how trustworthy and faithful He is. Off the cuff, God gave me the stories and verses I needed to teach. The women couldn't believe what they were seeing and hearing. I couldn't have prepared what He had prepared for me. There was never a better teacher on the planet than Jesus, and Holy Spirit led Him every time He taught. God was telling me to trust and see Him do the miracle.

Let the Holy Spirit do the teaching, the leading, the dreaming, the anointing, the orchestrating, the connecting, and the opening of doors. Planning when He said "no" would've been disobedience. His requests may not always make sense but they can be trusted.

To advance to where God is calling us, He needs us to operate from the place of presence rather than programs and to-do lists. Goals are more difficult to accomplish if we're not abiding in the presence of God while doing them. For example, let's say I was scheduled to speak and felt unsure of my message with only ten minutes remaining before speaking. I've found that abiding in the presence of God (in secret) for those ten minutes is much more profitable than cramming for ten minutes to study. God can do in five minutes what could take us weeks or years to accomplish in our own strength.

Walking in continual awareness of God being present with us gives us confidence in the waiting, hidden, pruning seasons. Our confidence is in the power of God to do what we can't. Confidence leads to contentment. While we are content in the day to day, He's behind-the-scenes orchestrating our promise.

Generally, contentment comes before calling. As we find contentment in the ordinary and remain obedient in the small things, we come closer to stepping into our destiny. The highway getting there is as important to God as the destination.

Don't try to force things. Pushing our way through, or strategically aligning ourselves with people because of where we think they can get us is manipulation. Doing things in our own strength, way, and time is making an agreement with the enemy and opening the door to possibly thwarting the actual plans God originally had for us. That's the exact thing the enemy wants to do. Pray for divine alignments, and then wait. In the words of Ryan LeStrange, "Let God divinely connect, reconnect, and disconnect you."

Never give up hope in the Author of Hope to heal what's sick, mend what's broken, and awaken dreams. Hope is how we inherit the promises of God, and belief gets to see them take shape. Hope allows us to see beyond this world into the Spirit one. There our dreams are already established, and we get to call them forth. Hope is our lifeline to faith, and faith fuels our destiny. Nothing, no thing, is too hard for God.

> *"May He grant you according to your heart's desire, and fulfill all your purpose." Psalm 20:4*

Prayer:
Father, Thank you for the perfect gift of your Son. Hope has a name. It's Jesus. No matter what life may be throwing our way, we choose today to place our hope and our trust in You, Jesus. Amen.

CHAPTER SEVEN

This Wild And Rushing River

"The river's deep, the river's wide, the river's water is alive. So sink or swim, I'm diving in."
~ Steven Curtis Chapman

RIVERS AND MOUNTAIN SPRINGS have always intrigued me. While in college in the North Carolina mountains, I frequented rivers for picnics and places to get away with God. When my husband and I lived in California, I loved visiting Yosemite National Park, particularly in spring. The snowmelt would cause the waterfalls and rivers to flow with forceful intensity. It was so loud anywhere in close proximity to either that two people couldn't hear themselves having a conversation. The falls roared with magnificent beauty and unrelenting power, so much so, an umbrella was needed to prevent being drenched.

The thing with rivers and waterfalls is they never stop—unless there's a severe drought. There's no switch to turn them off. From up higher, they are sourced with overflow and endless supply. The continual water flow and unstoppable force turns jagged-edged rocks into smooth ones.

This is the same with the Spirit of God. His beauty and power are incomparable, and His supply is unending. His love is passionate and untainted. We have nothing to fear. No matter how much or how little we know of God, there's always more. Our thoughts about Him should never be based solely on experience or what we've seen or heard from other people. He's not limited by our perceptions. Regardless of what we think of Him, He's still God, unchanging and flawless in all His ways.

River of Life

A plant drooping from drought will stand tall within an hour of being watered. Dry grass will turn green within a day of watering it. Our bodies and souls do the same. There's nothing finer than refreshing, cool water when your mouth is dry. It's a necessity.

> *"Jesus stood and cried out, saying, 'If anyone thirsts, let him come to Me and drink. He who believes in Me, as the Scripture has said, out of his heart will flow rivers of living water.' But this He spoke concerning the Spirit, whom those believing in Him would receive; for the Holy Spirit was not yet given, because Jesus was not yet glorified." John 7:37-39*

Without the Holy Spirit fueling us, our spirit will suffer. Jesus promised the refreshing, limitless supply of the Holy Spirit for those who believe. For the one who receives Him, out of his heart will flow rivers of living water. When we believe and open ourselves up to Him, our innermost being will overflow with the water of the Spirit who gives life to weary, dried-up, dying souls.

As often as possible, I would stop by the local store and encourage my friend with truth. I was shocked when Curtis announced he had become a Christian. I had been talking to him about Jesus off and on for several years. In return, he had argued why He didn't believe in God and how the Bible was just a good book that makes us good citizens. After He started reading the Bible, everything changed. Through the gospels and the book of Acts (Acts of the Holy Spirit), he encountered God. The Holy Spirit began to woo and convict him. Jesus said:

> *"Nevertheless I tell you the truth. It is to your advantage that I go away; for if I do not go away, the Helper will not come to you; but if I depart, I will send Him to you. And when He has come, He will convict the world of sin, and of righteousness, and of judgment: of sin, because they do not believe in Me; of righteousness, because I go to My Father and you see Me no more; of judgment, because the ruler of this world is judged." John 16:7-11*

Curtis later shared how he had a few days when his wife was out of town with their babies. He fasted, read the Bible, and prayed during those days alone with God. He spent much of that time on his knees, repenting of sin and asking for forgiveness. Immersed in truth and the presence of God, inevitably, he was changed. After receiving Jesus as His Savior, the life-giving water of God's Spirit drenched his weary soul. Rather than being weighed down, now when I see Curtis, he is so alive and full of joy.

The River Rising

Ezekiel was alone with God in Ezekiel 40, when God took him up to a high mountain overlooking Israel and gave Him a vision. Ezekiel had a perspective shift that day. He got to go up and see from God's view. Taken to the entrance of the city, he met a man there with the appearance of brass. The man was Ezekiel's tour guide through his vision. Many Bible scholars believe the man was Jesus, who had feet of brass when He was seen by John, as recorded in Revelation 1:15. The man told Ezekiel to open his eyes, ears, and mind to everything he was going to see and to declare it to Israel.

During the vision, Ezekiel was taken to the door of the temple. Water flowed from the threshold of the temple on the right side toward the east. At the east gate the water was trickling as it flowed east. The man led Ezekiel eastward. As the man measured off equal distances, the water was at first ankle deep, then knee deep and then up to his waist. The man of brass measured, and soon the river was so deep it could not be crossed. They stood along the bank of the river and noticed trees lining both sides. The man told him the river flowed to the sea, and after reaching the sea, its (the sea's) waters were healed. Flowing from God's temple, everything the river touched was healed (Ezekiel 47).

> *"And it shall be that every living thing that moves, wherever the rivers go, will live. There will be a very great multitude of fish, because these waters go there; for they will be healed, and everything will live wherever the river goes." (verse 9)*

Along the banks of the river fishermen would come, and there were fish in abundance. Many trees grew there and were used for food. Their leaves stayed green through drought, they produced fruit, and their leaves were used for medicine. The swamps would be given over to salt, but the river brought life and healing.

> *"But its swamps and marshes will not be healed; they will be given over to salt. Along the bank of the river, on this side and that, will grow all kinds of trees used for food; their leaves will not wither, and their fruit will not fail. They will bear fruit every*

month, because their water flows from the sanctuary. Their fruit will be for food, and their leaves for medicine." (verse 11-12)

I was never hugely fond of my name growing up, because it was so different. I wanted a name I could find on a personalized keychain. I've never met another person with the first name Rivera. Unless they had met me, most people would never know I'm a Caucasian, southern girl who loves wide-open spaces and homemade biscuits and gravy.

According to an old Indian gentleman, Rivera means "river of life." Now that's a name I can live with: "*a river whose streams shall make glad the city of God.*" I never want to be a stagnant reservoir, holding onto all that's been poured into me. As a conduit of His Spirit and river of love, I want to gush out living water. God's Spirit gives us the ability to bring life and hope to everything and everyone we contact. When God is in the midst of us, we shall not be moved by circumstances or trauma, but will rather forge through them, like a mighty river.

> *"There is a river whose streams shall make glad the city of God, The holy place of the tabernacle of the Most High. God is in the midst of her, she shall not be moved. God shall help her, just at the break of dawn." Psalm 46:4-5*

As I read Ezekiel's vision of the river rising, I am reminded of the scene in "The Lord of the Rings: The Two Towers," when the trees woke up and began walking and talking. The hobbits climbed up and rode into battle in the top of a tree. From high up, they scanned across the valley basin for insight. The entire forest of huge trees rallied. Their higher, broader perspective allowed those little hobbits to enter into battle with confidence; meanwhile the ancient trees became heroes.

The children of God are the trees lining the river of God's Spirit. We are oaks of righteousness, plantings of the Lord (Isaiah 60). It's our privilege to tap into the river with our roots to carry hope and healing to others. There are people all over the world, like Curtis, who are anxiety ridden, hopeless, and in need of a Savior. Covering the banks of the river, rallying in battle, and carrying the good news, we stand tall as oaks of the Lord. With the spiritual food and medicine to heal, we bring the gospel message, and the Spirit brings conviction. We carry His presence with us wherever we go, and everything we touch is given life, hope and promise.

As the trees along the sides of the river link roots, it is a joy to link arms with our brothers and sisters. No drought can deter us, no storm can tear us down, and we are a fortress in battle. We are the prayer warriors, the messengers of truth, the moms who teach their children, the caregivers who care with precision, the givers whose gifts last a lifetime, and the encouragers whose words never fall to the ground. We are the army of God, strong and mighty in the strength of the Lord. May we always give what we've been so generously given.

Diving In

"I want the presence of God Himself, or I don't want anything at all to do with religion... I want all that God has or I don't want any." – A.W. Tozer

Often people are uncomfortable teaching and receiving teachings on the Holy Spirit. There's a hush in the room at the mere mention of the name. There's a lot of fear of the unknown and concern over loss of control associated with it. Most of us want comfort, so we come up with a version of God with which we're comfortable. Wanting nothing too out of the ordinary we prefer to keep God nice and tidy. We desire to put Him away and just bring Him out when it's convenient. This has never worked. If it has worked, perhaps it's not truly been God we've been dealing with. He's much too big for neat packages, especially ones of human-size thinking.

I vividly remember the first time I heard someone pray in their Holy Spirit prayer language. Many questions surfaced, and I was uncertain of what I was hearing. It made me a little nervous, because I didn't know if it was really from God. I asked questions, and that moment in time started me on a new journey with God—one where I would settle for nothing less than the truth. I had never been taught about the gifts of the Spirit. Many in the church believe those gifts were for Biblical times but not for today. I had never quite understood this school of thought since God hasn't changed. He's the Alpha and Omega, the First and the Last (Revelation 1). He's the same, yesterday, today and forever (Hebrews 13:8). If He hasn't changed, then why would His ability to give gifts or perform miracles?

The character and attributes of God are unchanging: Gift giver, Healer, Savior, Peace, Light of the World, Bread of Life, the Lord Our Righteousness, Provider, God Who Sees, the Word who became flesh, Deliverer, God of miracles, King of kings and Lord of lords, the One who was, and is and is to come, the One who makes impossible things possible and is perfect in all His ways. My basis for knowledge about anything having to do with His gifts, especially the gift of tongues or even having a private Spirit prayer language, was mostly what people had told me and the little I had studied on my own. I really needed Him to show me.

This was difficult, because I have a tendency to want to have all the answers. Like most humans, I also like to feel a certain amount of control over my situation. Submitting my mind to the Spirit of God was tough. If it didn't make sense with my mind, I wanted no part of it. But, I also knew I wanted everything God had for me. I still do. I knew I didn't want to miss it. The only way I could receive fully any gift He might have for me was to learn to let go and realize I couldn't control or understand everything about God and His ways. Most importantly, I had to learn to trust Him above myself.

I began to pray, "Lord if there's something about You that I've missed or learned wrong, change my mind. Show me." That's a difficult prayer to pray. Inviting God to change our minds is risky. It requires total submission to Holy Spirit, and trading the way we've always understood Him for His understanding. Since I started praying that prayer, this journey of getting to know the Spirit of God more intimately has been one of the most exciting times of my life.

Going Deeper

The height of God's glory and love are limitless, and His creative genius inspiring. He can speak through most anything. Our eyes and ears just need to be attuned to Him.

> *"For God may speak in one way, or in another, yet man does not perceive it. In a dream, in a vision of the night, when deep sleep falls upon men, while slumbering on their beds, Then He opens the ears of men, and seals their instruction." Job 33:14-16*

It fascinates me that God talks to me in my sleep. I guess it's easier for me to hear Him at that time. My mind and reasoning are slowed down so-to-speak. For example, I dreamed once of being in the middle of the ocean in the dark. I looked up and saw a huge bridge with a tsunami-like wave rising up under the bridge. The dream changed scenes, and I was body surfing this wave with ease. It was so real. I could feel the air and water hitting my face. The wave carried me toward a big city with lights.

The dream had multiple meanings, but one thing I believe God was pointing out to me was the tsunami was a wave of His glory and the coming revival in the land. As I spent time asking God what He was trying to reveal to me personally, He said, "Rivera, you can't ride a wave at all, if you're not willing to go into the deep. No one has ever caught a wave by standing on the shore." I knew I had to step into the deep with Him to ever be found on top of that wave.

Growing up vacationing at the beach, my daddy would take me into the deep water to teach me to float. I learned then that going into the deep required a great deal of trust. I had to trust that my daddy's hands were there to catch me if I started to sink. The same day God spoke to me about the deep, He took me to scripture where Jesus says:

> *"Launch out into the deep and let down your nets for a catch."*
> *Luke 5:4b*

Peter was told to go into the deep. He reasoned that they had been fishing in that spot all night. In that moment, Peter had to choose to trust. Then he said, *"...at Your word, I'll let down the net."* Basically he was saying, because you say so I'll do it, even though I don't understand it. Because of blind obedience to launch into the deep, Peter got to experience the miracle. They caught so many fish their net was breaking, and they had to ask their partners in another boat to help them. They filled both boats until they were so full they began to sink. Peter was astonished and bowed down at Jesus' feet to worship. As I read the story, God wanted me to see this next.

> *"And Jesus said to Simon (Peter), 'Do not be afraid. From now on you will catch men.'" Luke 5:10b*

God will give us what we need most, even when we're unsure of what it is. Nothing is too difficult for God, whether it's a net filled with fish or revelation about our own journey with Him. Peter was loaded down with fish and downloaded with the revelation that he would be a fisher of men.

Fear not. Trust. Go where I tell you. Do what I tell you. You will witness many miracles. You will see My glory. We have to be willing to face our fears to see and be a part of the signs and wonders of God. Only God is capable of loading us down with a miracle while downloading us with revelation through it. Splashing in the deep waters of His Spirit, we experience the depths of His love.

Perfect Gifts For Imperfect People

"If you then, being evil, know how to give good gifts to your children, how much more will your heavenly Father give the Holy Spirit to those who ask Him!" Luke 11:13

Most of us have either been a part of, or witnessed, families fighting over money surrounding the death of a loved one. As a nurse, I once cared for the mother of a prominent California family. It was sickening to watch as the children brought in lawyers at separate times. They were each trying to be the last to get their mother to sign papers, leaving her money to them.

A similar thing happens in the church. We compare, judge and have division over the gifts our Father has so graciously given through His Spirit. We have each been apportioned gifts according to His will and good pleasure. Yet we want more, or we judge others for what they've been given.

When I mention gifts of the Spirit, I'm referring to those described in 1 Corinthians 12: word of wisdom, word of knowledge, faith, the gift of healing, the working of miracles, prophecy, discerning of spirits, different kinds of tongues, and the interpretation of tongues.

"But one and the same Spirit works all these things, distributing to each one individually as He wills." 1 Corinthians 12:11

Our Father wants us to each have a child's part. He wants us to receive our inheritance, but so many won't accept His gifts and then many judge those who do. It's sad that the family of God is divided over the gifts of the Spirit, particularly the gift of tongues. Speaking in tongues is one of the most controversial subjects in the church. Not just whether it's for today but whether it is for everyone.

There are so many schools of thought on this subject. We are divided over a gift. What difference does it really make, if we all love Jesus? If some choose to receive and some don't, should it really matter? Shouldn't we be unified on what matters most, and lay our opinions down for the sake of being family? I realize many gifts have been misused. Sometimes misuse has been due to zeal with spiritual immaturity, like what was happening in the Corinthian church. But we should be careful that we aren't being too quick to decide what's genuine and what isn't. I also realize there is power and joy from the Spirit when we receive His gifts.

About five years ago, I gave my husband an anniversary card. I later found it, unopened, in his bedside drawer. I quickly learned he's not a "words" guy, and he could care less about cards. At least he put it in safekeeping. I'm not offended, but I wonder how many years it will take him to open the card and find the money I placed inside? No matter how badly we may want people to receive and open their gifts, we can't force it. God won't force it either. That's why it's called a gift. All the confusion and misunderstanding over this subject is a huge tool of the enemy. He wants to cause division in the church and keep us from walking in the fullness of what God has for us.

Once in a meeting of racial and denominational diversity, I said, "I

95

love seeing people from so many church backgrounds come together in unity to worship. God loves it even more. Inevitably when people of varying backgrounds come together, we may not agree on everything. If you happen to hear someone praying in their prayer language during these meetings, don't be offended. What they're praying is between them and God. It has nothing to do with you. Or maybe it does. They just might be praying for you." Laughter filled the room. It was so refreshing to have women open their hearts to women who may have had a slightly different interpretation of the Word than they did. None of us are God. Ask Him to search your heart and reveal things to you that can only be revealed by His Spirit.

> *"But as it is written: 'Eye has not seen, nor ear heard, Nor have entered into the heart of man The things which God has prepared for those who love Him.' But God has revealed them to us through His Spirit. For the Spirit searches all things, yes, the deep things of God." 1 Corinthians 2:9-10*

Gifts of the Spirit should always operate from a place of love. Fruit of the Spirit and gifts should go hand in hand. One should never be without the other. If a person is operating in gifts but there's no evidence of fruit, then the authenticity of the gifts could be in question. Jesus undeniably exemplified gifts with fruit. He encompassed all the gifts and fruit. He is the gift.

Power From on High

> *"Behold, I send the Promise of My Father upon you; but tarry in the city of Jerusalem until you are endued with power from on high." Luke 24:49*

> *"He [Jesus] commanded them [the disciples] not to depart from Jerusalem, but to wait for the Promise of the Father, 'which,' He*

said, 'you have heard from Me; for John truly baptized with water, but you shall be baptized with the Holy Spirit not many days from now... But you shall receive power when the Holy Spirit has come upon you; and you shall be witnesses to Me in Jerusalem, and in all Judea and Samaria, and to the end of the earth.'" Acts 1:4-5, 8

The disciples waited. They met. They prayed. Days passed, and they continued to wait. Jesus knew they would be preaching the gospel and praying for the sick to be made well, but without the infusion of His Spirit, their efforts would be powerless.

"And suddenly there came a sound from heaven, as of a rushing mighty wind, and it filled the whole house where they were sitting. Then there appeared to them divided tongues, as of fire, and one sat upon each of them. And they were all filled with the Holy Spirit and began to speak with other tongues, as the Spirit gave them utterance." Acts 2:2-4

Being endued with power from on high is what we call the baptism of the Holy Spirit. The simplest description of baptism is from the Greek word: baptizō (G907), which means to submerge, to cleanse, and to overwhelm.

Whereas John's baptism is being submerged in water, Jesus' baptism is being immersed in the Spirit. With water baptism we go under water and then we're lifted back out. This is symbolic of dying to our old way of living and being raised into a new life in Christ. Jesus exemplified this when he had John baptize Him. John the Baptist spoke about this in Matthew 3:11.

"I indeed baptize you with water unto repentance, but He [Jesus] who is coming after me is mightier than I, whose sandals

*I am not worthy to carry. He will baptize you with the Holy
Spirit and fire."*

Jesus' baptism is one of the Spirit coming down from on high and
saturating us with an endless supply. It's powerful. Like fire is all
consuming and burns anything in its path, this baptism with Holy
Spirit and fire is one of consumption. When it happens, we are
overcome with the Spirit. God pours out His love, power and gifts on
us in an immeasurable and often uncontrollable way. It's undeniably
God when it happens. When we've been baptized, or saturated with
God's Spirit, we carry a supernatural ability or anointing to do what
we could not do in our own strength. We become so immersed with
the Spirit that His ability overrides ours.

Right after he commissioned the disciples to go into all the world
making disciples and baptizing them, Jesus said: *"And these signs will
follow those who believe: In My name they will cast out demons; they will
speak with new tongues; they will take up serpents; and if they drink
anything deadly, it will by no means hurt them; they will lay hands on
the sick, and they will recover." Mark 16:17*

These signs will follow those who believe. That's it. Whether we believe.
We have to ask ourselves if we really believe God. I'm afraid many of
us have tried to limit God by fitting Him into our way of thinking,
rather than trusting Him even when we can't wrap our minds around
Him. I don't think Jesus was implying that we drink poison to test
God's ability to save. I do think He was indicating that we step into the
realm of the miraculous when we believe.

Once I was in a meeting at a church food pantry where people had
come to receive groceries, a message, worship, prayer, or whatever
they might need. There were four people seated together in a row.
One of the ladies motioned for me to come near. As I approached

them, she told me she needed prayer for her neck. She was in pain, so I asked her to believe with me in prayer. Healing is interesting because we never know who God is going to heal. It's not our job to figure it out. One of the keys to Him healing is faith. So it's our job to show up, ask, and believe. He will do the rest. He alone will shift what needs to shift to bring the healing, whether it's cells in the human body or mindsets.

We briefly prayed for healing in Jesus' name, and her neck pain started disappearing. Another woman in the group witnessed what had happened, so she asked for prayer for a different body part. I laid my hands gently on her, and we prayed God would heal her as well. She was healed. This happened two more times with the other two. The whole group experienced healing from God. From my experience as a critical care nurse, I knew one of the ways I could gauge the progress of their healing was by measuring their pain levels. They each had a different pain, but it was mostly outward and muscular, so the difference in pain could be measured right away.

To receive from God in this way, we must believe. One of the reasons I believe God wants to heal is because He healed me. I was diagnosed with Crohn's disease more than 20 years ago. I had some physical complications as a result. I never talked about what was going on with my body. I refused to walk in sickness or be defined by it. I refused to own it. According to doctors, this particular problem would never heal without surgery. Even with surgery, healing wasn't guaranteed. I had dealt with these complications for about five years.

One night while lying in bed, I was in pain but I prayed, "Jesus, I believe You and ask You to heal me. By Your stripes I am healed. Will you please heal me?" This prayer continued for quite a while when I felt warmth come across my torso. The ailment I had experienced for five years disappeared and has never returned. I've since gone to several follow-ups with my doctor. Each time he's looked inside my body, he has said there are no indications of Crohn's. The fact that he diagnosed me is the only way he knows I ever had it. He asked what I had been doing different. I told him nothing. I believed and prayed, and then Jesus healed me.

Holy Spirit communicates with our spirits, not our intellect. If we wait until we can wrap our minds around the Spirit to receive the more He wants to give us, we will miss it. We must go higher with God to gain His perspective and mine nuggets of truth and revelation from His Word. He will teach us who He is. God will show us what we've missed, if only we're willing to surrender our finite minds and limited ideas to His Spirit. Every gift from the Spirit is designed to glorify God and make Him visible on the earth, and should always be fueled by love.

Holy Spirit is not an experience, He's a person—the One who leads, guides, and convicts. He shows us how to pray and praise. He speaks to us, Spirit to spirit, and was sent to point to Jesus. He hears what's on God's heart and reveals it to us. He's a gentleman and a warrior, kind and bold simultaneously. Waterfalls of His presence empower from above, stirring us deeper in knowledge, wisdom and revelation of God and ourselves.

He allows us to be mighty trees fed by the river of His delights, endowing us with gifts to see the sick healed and the lost saved. He loves us outrageously. We can't comprehend it fully and trying to contain it would be like attempting to hold the ocean in one hand. It simply can't be done. How freeing and fun to float wherever this wild and rushing river of His presence chooses to take us.

Prayer:
Jesus, Thank you for the gift of Holy Spirit. We choose to open ourselves up to all that you have for us. We don't want to miss a thing. Any gift you want to give, we open our hands and hearts to

receive. We choose to trust you. We choose to float in the deep waters of intimacy with you knowing your strong arms are there to catch us. We rest in you. Give us the more you have for us. We want all of you, God. Fill and empower us with your Spirit. Saturate us with Your presence. In Jesus' name. Amen.

CHAPTER EIGHT

Circle Of Fire

*"All the darkness in the world cannot
extinguish the light of a single candle."*
~ St. Francis of Assisi

SEVERAL YEARS AGO, I had a dream. I was standing on the side of a mountain in a clearing. I could see over the top of trees, and beyond them the ocean was visible. Standing with me, in this several acre-sized clearing was a huge circle of people dressed in colorful outfits. They looked as though they were leaders of different people groups, or tribes of different nations. Each one of them was holding a torch. None of their torches were lit. I was holding a torch in my right hand, and it had fire and smoke on the end of it. I used my torch to light the person's torch to my right. That one lit the next person's torch and the process continued until the entire circle was lit.

The fire and smoke represented the power and move of the Holy Spirit. The circle symbolized covenant with God and unity among diverse people groups. This dream indicated a calling and move of the Spirit that will bring unity and influence leaders of nations. I knew this dream was specific to my life but I believe what God says to me is often a message to His Bride. So this dream was for you as well.

We should never underestimate the power of our influence. As we stop to light one torch at a time, the world is changed one person at a time.

> *"You are the light of the world. A city that is set on a hill cannot be hidden. Nor do they light a lamp and put it under a basket, but on a lampstand, and it gives light to all who are in the house. Let your light so shine before men, that they may see your good works and glorify your Father in heaven." Matthew 5:14-16*

Our lives are the sum total of many brief moments. Choices. People. Situations. Words. An encounter with a total stranger. One encouraging word or an unexpected promotion can change the trajectory of a life in seconds. Our presence can be a "suddenly" in someone's life. A suddenly is being in the right place at the right time to make an unexpected connection or to see the fulfillment of a promise from God. We can bring light to situations and conversations. Every doctor's appointment, grocery line, or child's ballgame is an opportunity. As moms and dads, whether we realize it or not, we lead. Our daily decisions affect other's lives. Most of us have siblings, cousins, nieces or nephews. Our lives are being watched. Whether positive or negative, every human has influence. We're all connected to someone, whether family, friends, neighbors, or coworkers.

> *"You are our epistle written in our hearts, known and read by all men; clearly you are an epistle of Christ, ministered by us, written not with ink but by the Spirit of the living God, not on tablets of stone but on tablets of flesh, that is,*

of the heart." 2 Corinthians 3:2-3

We are living letters, written by the Spirit of God. One flame of God's love can light up a heart, and in turn ignite an entire family, region, or country.

When Leaders Lead

Two of the most influential evangelists of our generation, Reinhard Bonnke and Billy Graham, have led millions to Jesus. They are leaders among leaders, completely surrendered to the guidance of the Holy Spirit. They've been anointed by the Spirit to go beyond human ability. Surrendered to His call, no matter the sacrifice, they believed God emphatically and prayer was always priority.

Ezra, Nehemiah, Esther, Haggai, Zechariah, and Zerubbabel were contemporaries. They were common people made mighty by God. He chose to align and strategically position them to carry out His plans in the time in which they lived. Ezra, a writer, teacher and priest, led Jews previously exiled to Babylon back to Jerusalem. He was given the job of teaching the Word of God to the people in Jerusalem. Esther was positioned in power as a Jewish Queen in Persia. She interceded on behalf of her people and helped save the Jews from plans to annihilate them. Meanwhile, Nehemiah, who had been serving as the cupbearer to a king in a foreign land, was commissioned by God to gather a team and rebuild the wall around Jerusalem. Haggai and Zechariah were prophets, and Zerubbabel was the governor appointed to rebuild the temple.

All of these individuals had several qualities in common. Each was chosen, anointed, and willing. There was a divine alignment that had to take place for each of them to accomplish their destinies. They carried an anointing to do a new thing and to break through the resistance of the enemy. This is often referred to as having a breaker anointing. Jesus *is* the breaker anointing. When we follow Him closely, we will have a breakthrough anointing too. We can learn a great deal from the leadership of Jesus and these great men and women of God.

> *"The one who breaks open will come up before them; They will break out, Pass through the gate, and go out by it; their king will pass before them, with the Lord at their head." Micah 2:13*

Prayer and Passion

Let's look at Nehemiah for example:

> *"And they said to me, 'The survivors who are left from the captivity in the province are there in great distress and reproach. The wall of Jerusalem is also broken down, and its gates are burned with fire.' So it was, when I heard these words, that I sat down and wept, and mourned for many days; I was fasting and praying before the God of heaven." Nehemiah 1:3-4*

Nehemiah was ignited by his awareness of the injustice done to his people. He was passionate as he saw beyond what was to what could be. He began to turn his face toward heaven, seeking God first. He asked for forgiveness from God and favor with men to accomplish the task. He said:

> *"I pray, Lord God of heaven, O great and awesome God, You who keep Your covenant and mercy with those who love You and observe Your commandments, please let Your ear be attentive and Your eyes open, that You may hear the prayer of Your servant which I pray before You now, day and night." Nehemiah 1:5-6a*

His relationship with God was genuine. He didn't go to God just for what he could get from Him. He was yielded to God, listening to Him before giving an answer to the king.

> *"Then the king said to me, 'What do you request?' So I prayed to the God of heaven. And I said to the king, 'If it pleases the king, and if your servant has found favor in your sight, I ask that you send me to Judah, to the city of my fathers' tombs, that I may rebuild it.'" Nehemiah 2:4-5*

Nehemiah went to the king as a humble servant. He was a leader, willing to serve alongside those he led and those who led him.

Vision and Encouragement

Nehemiah identified the problem and then cast his vision to the king. God gave Nehemiah such favor with King Artaxerxes that the king gave Nehemiah permission to rebuild the wall. The king also provided what was needed for the rebuilding project. Once given the go-ahead from the king, Nehemiah was focused. He was a man on a mission.

A.W. Tozer once said: "God is looking for people through whom He can do the impossible. What a pity we plan to do only the things that we can do by ourselves."

Often it's true. We get a vision but forget to bring people along to join us. Or we choose to do the things small enough to accomplish them on our own. Nehemiah knew the value of help. He knew he couldn't go at it alone, so he cast the same vision to the people he had presented to the king. Right away he had workers who came alongside him to help. This trustworthy, humble leader presented a notable cause and people were on board.

> *"Where there is no vision, the people perish [die]." Proverbs 29:18a (KJV)*

People want to be part of something bigger than themselves that will make a positive difference in the world. Encourage them. Bring them along with you, and catapult them beyond their wildest dreams. How many of us are one Barnabas from being a world changer? We all need a Paul and a Timothy. We all need someone alongside us to encourage us and pull out the greatness in us. Meanwhile, we should do the same for others.

Nehemiah was one of the greatest leaders in history. As an equipper and encourager, he positioned others to be great. He placed them where they could succeed, in positions of their greatest strength. Nehemiah was willing to work as hard as those alongside him. Obviously he had to delegate, but he didn't ask anyone to do what he wasn't willing to do himself. Coming off the wall was non-negotiable. Nehemiah knew if he did, the work would slow down. Nothing was worth getting off course, so he continued working as hard, if not harder, than everyone on the assignment.

> *"So I sent messengers to them, saying, 'I am doing a great work, so that I cannot come down. Why should the work cease while I leave it and go down to you?'" Nehemiah 6:3*

With focus and determination, Nehemiah led a movement that rebuilt an enormous wall out of ruins. They *"loaded themselves so that with one hand they worked at construction, and with the other held a weapon" (Nehemiah 4:17)*. They worked in shifts around the clock and were willing to fight when necessary to maintain steady progress. God honored Nehemiah by placing people around him to do what he couldn't do alone.

Nehemiah needed help, and hundreds of people came alongside him. This is a picture of the Body being the body. Every limb and organ is needed in its place for the entire body to function properly. A project this big—building a wall around a city—could never have been completed if he'd tried to do it alone. Because of God's favor and Nehemiah's leadership, people were more than willing to help. They caught the vision, and in 52 days the wall around Jerusalem was rebuilt. When their enemies heard or saw that the wall was finished in 52 days, they realized it was a miracle from God.

During the process of writing this book, I had an army of people around me. I was physically alone, but I had support. Family and friends had weapons in one hand and hammers in the other to help make this possible. Some have worked in a physical way, helping my family while I have been gone. Others have fought by praying me through every single day. Then there were voices of reason, truth and encouragement when I wanted to give up. I couldn't do this without them, and God knew it.

Confident, secure friends, who don't make comparisons, are invaluable in this life. They are the ones with eyes and hearts on what God wants. All of our God assignments are different, but how sweet when we can spur one another along and help see each other through the struggles to the promise. When we can't lay down comparison and celebrate one another's successes, we're not ready for our own. Pray for and encourage one another. Surround yourself with God-confident, kingdom-minded, selfless people. Ask and God will send them. Just as trees in the forest grow with their roots intertwined and are able to weather the storms, together we can accomplish more than we ever would've dreamed of doing on our own.

An Army Arising

We are living in a time unlike any other in history, the eleventh hour. In these last days, Jesus will return for His Bride. Justice will have its way. A fearless generation is upon us. An army of sold-out fire starters is being raised up and released. What an honor to witness it, much less help lead in it. I recently had the privilege of being a part of the leadership team for a school for young revivalists in Wilmington, North Carolina. High school and college students from across the United States were represented at Wildfires School. Everyone, including those leading, was inspired by God. Flames were fanned, dreams birthed, and leaders activated. God spoke clearly and miracles occurred, impacting all. Empowered by the Holy Spirit to be radical carriers of God's love and truth, the young ones released this year are as bold as wild horses running in the wind, unhindered and unstoppable.

Reinhard Bonnke said: "Jesus did not call them—or you and me—to ditch their smiles and to wear sackcloth. His mission was not to turn people into 'stick-in-the-muds.' Jesus Himself was not very conventional! The disciples caught His infectious spirit, one that would challenge the stuffy establishment. He showed them new things, especially faith and love, by which, they would conquer the world."

Many in the world are tired of hearing about God and would rather see Him. The world needs to experience the love of Jesus firsthand. If people witness God through miracles accompanied by genuine love, they will inevitably be changed. We may be the only Bible someone will read. Most of the world has never been to church and we get to take them. We are the church. They will go to church when we leave the building. May we choose to live in a way that when people run into us on the streets or in the supermarket, they have experienced church (the Ecclesia of God) and encountered Jesus. When we as the Body begin to live in this way, God is going to pour out His Spirit to reveal Himself in signs, wonders, and miracles like never before.

At the wedding party in John 2, Jesus told his mother His time had not yet come (for public ministry), when she suggested He do something about the wine shortage. Mary believed in Him. I wonder what she had seen Him do as He was growing up. Imagine the insight she had from being His mother. Like any mother, she was excited to show him off to the world, and Jesus' plans shifted in that moment. There was a divine realignment. He honored his earthly mother and performed His first public miracle by turning water into wine. When Jesus did so, it was not just any old wine, but the most quality wine.

To those at the wedding who knew nothing of the miracle, it appeared the best wine had been saved for last. God has a way of saving the best for last. The last shall be first and the first shall be last. If you've been waiting for your miracle or the fulfillment of His promise, it's a time of new wine. Quality new wine. If new wine is put into an old wineskin, it will crack and burst open. We need new wineskins, or new mindsets and ways of doing things, in this hour. We will have to lay down our traditions and what's seemingly worked in the past to live in fresh revelation and creativity from God as we move forward.

His goodness hasn't changed. His Word hasn't changed. God Himself hasn't changed. But He may lead us with new strategy and experiences from heaven to reach the world in which we are navigating. God has saved the best wine for last. We have the privilege of living in this time to see His glory made manifest on earth! Not only that, we get to be His sent ones to share the "good news!" We are entering into a new season and territory. This era is one of ushering in the kingdom of God on earth!

Over the last couple of years God has been speaking to me a lot about being "as His mouth," representing Him through speaking. He takes me frequently to scriptures about His fire. It can't be contained or quenched.

"Son of man, set your face to the South and preach against the South and prophesy…say…'hear the word of the Lord, "Behold, I will kindle a fire in you, and it shall devour every green tree and every dry tree in you; the blazing flame shall not be quenched, and all faces from the south to the north shall be scorched by it. All flesh shall see that I, the Lord, have kindled it; it shall not be quenched.""" Ezekiel 20:46-48

We are called to ready the Bride of Christ: calling in the lost to salvation, the sick to healing, freedom for the prisoners, and deliverance for those bound (Isaiah 61/Luke 4)! The Bride is waking up and realizing who she is and of what she's capable by the power of the Spirit. A shift has occurred.

Divine Assignment and Alignment

Our yes is valuable to God. Humanly speaking, nothing qualifies us to do what only He can do. If we are saved, we're called. God qualifies those He calls. He prepares those who are willing. He's assigning some of us to new things in this hour. There's a recalibration and reset occurring to ready his sent ones for new assignments, territories and direction. Faith and willingness to step out are basic and most essential to us seeing His miracles.

"The people who know their God shall be strong and carry out great exploits." Daniel 11:32b

Prior to helping with Wildfires School, I had been asking God why He was sending me to be a part of their leadership. Up to that point, my role in ministry had been primarily with women, mostly in the church. Working with teens, college and career-aged adults seemed a little out of the norm for me. Because God had confirmed me going, I thought, "What in the world are You doing, Lord? What do you want from me for this school, God?"

I heard Him say, "Humility. Do whatever they ask you to do, and do it with a grateful heart."

When I was growing up in the church, I was taught women could only have influence with other women, or children. I rarely witnessed men and women working together to lead. Women mostly taught Sunday school and provided casseroles for potlucks, while men occupied the teaching and leadership positions. I had never felt the freedom to venture outside of speaking only to women because of my background. Besides, I had known for years I was called to women and knew there was a grace on my life to influence them.

Weeks before the school, leadership asked me to speak to all the students and staff during the school on outreach day. As I prepared to speak, God gave me a specific word. As the school week progressed, I noticed the message God had given me was already being spoken at different points. I began to question whether I was to give that specific message. Leadership encouraged me that the message should be given, because I would bring it from a woman's heart. It was true that men had done most of the teaching. I agreed bringing a new perspective would shift things a little.

The same morning I was to teach, someone was asked to give a devotion, which went a little longer than expected. I suggested to leadership that it wasn't necessary for me to speak. They were gracious and agreed. Instead of teaching what I had prepared, I was asked to share briefly about the Holy Spirit and hearing the voice of God. So I did.

Since it was a revivalist school, they were holding meetings each night of that week. Each evening we would worship and hear a guest speaker, some from out of state. Wednesday night we had originally planned to be at the beach with students and staff. However, the host church had announced there would be meetings each evening, Monday through Friday. To honor their announcement, Wildfires leadership needed a speaker for Wednesday night. They asked me if I would speak, since I had bowed out of speaking for outreach as originally planned.

The shifting and realignment of the day left me speechless. Only He could have orchestrated the events of the day in this way. This was unexpected and what we would call a "suddenly." It was Wednesday morning when leadership had asked me to teach that evening. I said yes. After the busyness of the day, I had about an hour to pull His message together. Fortunately, in the wee hours of the mornings, Holy Spirit had been speaking to me in my alone times with Him. Unbeknownst to me, God was writing the message throughout that week. His message was powerful, and the Spirit of God moved in the hearts of people.

It was a message of unity, identity and authority. A focus of the message was the necessity of unity among races, denominations, generations, and gender. Unity was put on display. We witnessed what happens when we work together and value one another's strengths and callings. That night, Holy Spirit led, secure, mighty men of God put me on that platform. They knew their identity and were confident to partner with a woman called of God to speak. This couldn't have happened apart from their obedience and God's divine alignment.

In 2 Kings 5:2, Naaman's wife's servant girl unexpectedly found herself on assignment in a new territory:

> *"The Syrians had gone out on raids, and had brought back captive a young girl from the land of Israel. She waited on Naaman's wife."*

114

This young Israeli girl grew up believing in the God of miracles. She had been taken captive, away from her family and all she had known. Yet her faith remained strong in the living God: the One who parted the Red Sea, caused old ladies to have children, healed, saved, and delivered. There's no recorded name for this young girl. She may have felt insignificant, unseen, unnoticed, unimportant, and too young to make a difference. However, God saw her, knew her, and had written significant all over her life. What probably seemed like displacement was actually divine placement. She was right where God wanted her, and He was setting her up for success.

Naaman was a leper. This little Jewish girl knew if he could go see the prophet, Elisha, he would be healed. Regardless of her feelings, she spoke up and gave a valuable gift—information that would lead to his healing, first physical then spiritual.

> "Then she said to her mistress, "If only my master were with the prophet who is in Samaria! For he would heal him of his leprosy." (verse 3)

The power of her words, twenty to be exact, changed the trajectory of a man's life. Ultimately, he did go see Elisha and reluctantly followed his instructions to dip in the Jordan River seven times. When he did, His skin was restored to normal. He confessed:

> "Indeed, now I know that there is no God in all the earth, except in Israel." (verse 15b)

His life was changed forever. He had encountered the healing power of the miracle-working God of Israel. Naaman chose to follow God from that day on. This girl's willingness to be used by God changed a man and probably His entire family for generations to come.

Many of us feel insignificant and under qualified to do what God is

115

asking. Some people will accomplish great exploits for God and never be recognized by men. God is strategically positioning thousands of seemingly insignificant people for moments of great significance. Most won't be famous on earth for their accomplishments, but they are famous with God. It's so easy to get caught up in fame and building platforms and names. It's also easy to forget fame and earthly accomplishments are not what give us value. Our identity in Christ is unchanging, our assignments are not. When we confuse our assignment *from* God with our position *in* Him, we get in trouble. If we associate our identity with our assignments, when the assignment is over, we begin to have an identity crisis. Our assignment is separate from who we are as God's children. Seasons come and seasons go but the love of God for His children and His mark on us never will.

The morning I sat down to start writing this book, God took me to this verse to confirm He was with me.

> *"Not by might, nor by power, but by my spirit, Says the Lord of hosts." Zechariah 4:6*

Not by any ability or might on my part but by His Spirit, it would be accomplished. Greatness comes when the Spirit of God aligns and empowers us beyond our natural abilities. His call and our willingness to move are two of the most important qualifications to greatness. God can and will do what we can't, if we believe Him for it and are willing. If He's asked us to do it, He's already prepared the way. God's anointing on His calling for our lives is Him saying yes to our yes. He puts our yes on display and causes people to stand in awe of Him through it. The anointing of God is when God does through us what we can't do on our own. Remember, His voice and His Word will always align. He will never ask us to do something contrary to His Word or character. We may never fully comprehend the significance of our yes in small acts of obedience.

"For we are His workmanship, created in Christ Jesus for good works, which God prepared beforehand that we should walk in them." Ephesians 2:10

Don't underestimate the power of God to set the entire world ablaze through "nameless" people. We are being aligned for pivotal, destiny shaping moments. God sees and knows. We were created for this very moment. As we find ourselves possibly feeling displaced or unmarked, we are actually being divinely aligned. We are marked with His name for greatness. Many nations will be lit up with a move of the Spirit of God because of our willingness to say yes.

Prayer:
Father, Thank you for calling us and setting us apart for great exploits on this earth. We call forth Your will in heaven over our lives. Align and position us to make a difference for the better while it is still called today. Help us to intentionally use our places of influence to glorify Your name without fear of what people will think. Thank you for your intellect, wisdom and creativity to do and be what you have called us to . In Jesus' name. Amen

CHAPTER NINE

Those Who Have Ears, Let Them Hear

"Once upon a time there was a tasteful table set for a queen to be alone with her King. What a grand time they had as He spoke to her heart of hidden treasures and love so deep she could hardly contain it."
~ Rivera Douthit {Ponderings}

AFTER MY FAMILY RETURNED home from an action-packed visit to California I was so excited to sleep in my own bed again. I couldn't wait for a slower pace. Have you ever needed a vacation from your vacation? That's sort of how I felt. I told God before dozing off how I had missed my quiet times and couldn't wait to get to spend time with Him again. I really needed Him.

That next morning, a voice woke me up. I heard the words, "Are you hungry?" It was loud, audible and jolted me awake. I thought my husband was waking me. I sat up in bed and looked around. No one was in the bedroom with me, and my door was shut. It was so real I got up to look around in the house. No one was downstairs. I had heard God in my spirit. I went straight to my Bible eager to hear from Him again. As it opened, I glanced down and my eyes went to:

"Behold, I stand at the door and knock. If anyone hears My voice and opens the door, I will come in to him and dine with him, and he with Me." Revelation 3:20

I had heard the voice of God, sure enough! He was asking me if I was hungry, not for actual food, but for the spiritual food He wanted to give me. He was so sweet to remind me in His Word that He wants to dine with us. All we have to do is open the door to Him. That never gets old. No matter where we are in our journey with Him, there's always more. His well of living water never runs dry. His supply of bread never runs out, and He always surprises us with joy. Every time we encounter God again, it is brand new as if it was our first time encountering Him.

"Now to him who is able to do exceedingly abundantly above all we can ask or think, according to his power at work within us, to Him be glory in the church by Christ Jesus to all generations, forever and ever. Amen." Ephesians 3:20-21

He can do more by the power of His Spirit through us than we could ever imagine in our wildest dreams. We can dream oceanic-sized dreams, and He will do so much more. We can't even wrap our minds around Him or of what He is capable. Amazing is an understatement. He is limitless in possibility. He makes impossible things possible by just walking in the room. It's amazing how He invites us into secret places with Him where He has set a table for two. How delicious.

Hearing God's Voice

Throughout scripture God speaks. In Genesis 3:9, God was walking through the Garden of Eden looking for Adam, *"Then the Lord God called to Adam and said to him, 'Where are you?'"*

Relationship is God's design. He created us to fellowship with Him and with one another. We are wired for friendship! To encourage, to empathize, and to love one another requires careful listening and speaking. God created us to do the same with Him.

When God called Samuel, he heard the audible voice of God three times.

> *"Now the boy Samuel ministered to the Lord before Eli. And the word of the Lord was rare in those days; there was no widespread revelation. And it came to pass at that time, while Eli was lying down in his place, and when his eyes had begun to grow so dim that he could not see, and before the lamp of God went out in the tabernacle of the Lord where the ark of God was, and while Samuel was lying down, that the Lord called Samuel. And he answered, 'Here I am!' So he ran to Eli and said, 'Here I am, for you called me.*
>
> *And he said, 'I did not call; lie down again.' And he went and lay down.*
>
> *Then the Lord called yet again, 'Samuel!'*
>
> *So Samuel arose and went to Eli, and said, 'Here I am, for you called me.' He answered, 'I did not call, my son; lie down again.'*

(Now Samuel did not yet know the Lord, nor was the word of the Lord yet revealed to him.)

And the Lord called Samuel again the third time. So he arose and went to Eli, and said, 'Here I am, for you did call me.' Then Eli perceived that the Lord had called the boy." 1 Samuel 30:1-8

Some people think that for us to say we know what God is saying is putting words in his mouth. They would say we have to be careful, because we can't truly know what's on His heart. Of course we can. We're on His heart. People loving people is on His heart. We know His heart from the Word. God is good, true, right, pure, strong, just, loving, patient, kind, trustworthy, and the list goes on. Anything that aligns with His character also aligns with His heart. A religious mindset is one that believes we can't know what's on God's heart, or that we can't really hear God's voice to know what He's saying. The truth is that we absolutely can. Jesus said:

"My sheep hear My voice, and I know them, and they follow Me. And I give them eternal life, and they shall never perish; neither shall anyone snatch them out of My hand." John 10:27-28

To truly know God intimately, we have to know His voice. To truly know His voice, we have to know His Spirit. The Spirit of God is the voice and counsel of God. The Holy Spirit is God. They are One: Father, Son and Holy Spirit. Jesus said He only did what He heard His Father tell Him to do. Jesus heard the Father's voice through the Holy Spirit. When we've seen One, we've seen them all. When we've heard One, we've heard them all. Our God is three persons in One, each 100% God and equally God. God does not want us to be afraid to come near Him. He speaks to us through the person of the Holy Spirit. He's the Counselor. How will He counsel if He's silent? The way to have intimacy with God and hear His voice is by way of the Holy Spirit.

"But when he, the Spirit of truth, comes, he will guide you into all truth. He will not speak on his own; he will speak only what he hears, and he will tell you what is yet to come. He will bring glory to me by taking from what is mine and making it known to you." John 16:13-14

Practically Powerful

Often I will wake up in the middle of the night to pray. One particular night I couldn't settle back to sleep. I asked God if something was on His heart and how He wanted me to pray while I was awake. He said, "Israel. Pray for Israel." This wasn't a typical practice for me. I love Israel because He does, but I normally didn't make it a routine thing to pray for Israel. I wasn't sure what He specifically wanted me to pray, but I prayed. As I started, I felt an urgency to pray for safety. I said, "Protect Israel, Lord. Bless them. Keep everyone there safe."

The next day, I saw a social media post from a woman in Israel. She had written the post at the same time I was up praying in America. Hamas, the Palestinian Islamist group that controls the Gaza Strip, was sending rockets to attack Israel. There had been evacuations and bomb sirens sounding. This was the first time anything had been in the news (that I was aware of) about Israel being in any kind of danger. But God. He knew and summoned someone (probably many others) in the United States to get up to pray in the middle of the night for what was on His heart.

Hearing God is powerful. It's even more powerful when we respond to it. This is how the world is changed! The question most people ask is how do I know I'm hearing Him? There are several keys to hearing the voice of God.

Find solitude and quiet with Him! It's in stillness, not noise and chaos, that we tune our spiritual ears to hear the voice of God. Getting alone with Him is key.

Mark 4:33-34 says: *"And with many such parables He spoke the word to them as they were able to hear it. But without a parable He did not speak to them. And when they were alone, He explained all things to His disciples."*

When the disciples were alone with Jesus, He explained to them the word He had spoken. They were given revelation and deeper understanding in their private moments with Him. Jesus is calling us to come away into the secret place with Him where He will give wisdom concerning future decisions, meaning to important questions, insight into His heart on a matter, or clarity on His Word.

Human voices will drown out His voice. Learn to say no to human demands and yes to the Spirit. Begin a routine and set aside a quiet place to meet with Him. Have something available for writing. As you're distracted by your to-do list, jot down any thoughts for later. Refocus your attention and write down in your journal what He's saying. Writing how you've heard and seen Him will grow your faith and remind you of His faithfulness later.

Practice the presence of God. Routine times of being still before the Lord will cultivate an awareness of the Holy Spirit who dwells in you. This will align your heart to hear. Then pray that He would make you sensitive to His voice.

"Be still, and know that I am God." Psalm 46:10

He absolutely longs to communicate with you. You must believe it, otherwise you may not hear. Communication with God is Spirit to spirit. The Lord speaks to our spirits. We most often hear Him in words, thoughts and impressions. Sometimes we'll miss the leading of the Lord, thinking it's our own thoughts. I have a friend who always says she's not sure if what she heard was the Lord or a bad burrito. This is more common than not. When the Holy Spirit speaks to our spirit, our mind will translate it: "I think God wants me to..." Or "I think God is saying..." Be confident in this: God does speak to us in our own thoughts. He created our minds, will, emotions, and imaginations. He made all of these aspects of us in His image. If we were created to process information with these, He will use them as conduits to speak and for us to hear Him.

We are wired to receive from God in several ways. We hear, see, and/or feel. Hearers will say, "I heard God say...." Feelers will say, "I feel like God is saying..." or, "I felt___ when I walked in the room." A seer will say, "God showed me..." or "I saw...." Begin to ask God to identify to you how He is most likely speaking to you. Maybe it's a combination of ways. But however God speaks to you, it will always line up with His written Word.

Learn the art of listening. Great communicators know how to listen well. Being still, quiet, and then speaking back what has been spoken are qualities of a great listener. Listening to God's thoughts will guide you in how to pray. It may even change the direction of your time with Him.

> *"Give ear, O my people, to My law; incline your ears to the words of My mouth. I will open my mouth in a parable; I will utter dark sayings of old. Which we have heard and known, and our fathers have told us." Psalm 78:1-3*

> *"Incline your ear, and come to Me. Hear, and your soul shall live; And I will make an everlasting covenant with you--" Isaiah 55:3*

Give ear. Incline your ears. He will speak through other people, His Word, or circumstances. We just have to have our spirits heightened and aware. If we've been asking, we'll normally know when He's answering. Habakkuk does a great job of describing what to do when we hear a word from God.

> *"I will stand my watch And set myself on the rampart, And watch to see what He will say to me, And what I will answer when I am corrected.*
>
> *Then the Lord answered me and said: 'Write the vision and make it plain on tablets, that he may run who reads it. For the vision is yet for an appointed time; but at the end it will speak, and it will not lie. Though it tarries, wait for it; because it will surely come, It will not tarry. Behold the proud, his soul is not upright in him; but the just shall live by his faith.'" Habakkuk 2:1-4*

To summarize:

- ➢ Watch.
- ➢ See what He will say (listen).
- ➢ Answer if necessary.
- ➢ Write what you see or hear.
- ➢ Make sure it's plain and clear. Ask God for clarification if you don't understand. Ask for an explanation.
- ➢ Let it encourage and speak, "that he may run" who reads (or hears) it.
- ➢ Wait for it to come to pass.
- ➢ Be humble and just.
- ➢ Have faith. Believe God for the fulfillment of the promise.

Ask Him to reveal Himself. He will. Ask Him to nudge you when He's speaking and to help you hear.

Pray, "Lord, open my eyes to see you and ears to hear you. Make your Word come alive to me as I'm reading. Awaken my soul to know when you're speaking. Help me not just hear Your word but become it. Amen"

People are hungry for truth and encouragement from God. How will He tell us, if we can't hear Him? Ask Him to show you if what you're hearing aligns with His character and His Word. As you seek Him, His very presence will become your sustenance. His desires will become yours. He will minister to you so you can minister to others as an overflow of your friendship with Him.

Deep Calls to Deep

"Deep calls unto deep at the noise of Your waterfalls; All Your waves and billows have gone over me." Psalm 42:7

Intimacy with God is deep. His spirit penetrates the deepest, darkest crevices of our souls. He bypasses our human reasoning. Spirit to spirit, we hear Him. His spirit and ours intertwine in sweet fellowship.

In the most recent season of my life, God has done a new thing. He asked me to lay aside things I normally had done for Him, to just be with Him. I laid down official ministry roles to "come away" with Him in secret. During this season, I spent more time in my closet, listening in the dark, than I ever had in my life. It was hidden, quiet, and a little isolated, but I wouldn't trade it. How invaluable is the secret place. What happens in secret with God, He eventually puts on display. It's one of the ways others witness His glory through us. In that place of being alone with Him, He reveals Himself in fresh ways. Then we get to give away revelation we've received from Him there.

That happened when I had the privilege of spending several days in Shasta, California with a group of women. They were so hungry for God. They wanted to see, feel, touch, and learn to hear Him more clearly. They wanted to experience Him personally and intimately, and that's exactly what they did. When we enter into time with God wanting more of Him, He never denies us. It's always so fun for me to get to be a part of such a time. One of the greatest privileges of what I do is being able to introduce women to God in a new way and witness their minds and hearts shifting.

> *"The Lord will command His lovingkindness in the daytime, and in the night His song shall be with me." Psalm 42:8*

God's not limited in His ways of communicating. Rebecca and Fonda were sleeping in the same room during our weekend together. Encouraging them to invite the Holy Spirit into their sleep, I told the ladies to wake up and write down any dreams or words from God they might hear in the night.

> *"For God may speak in one way, or in another, yet man does not perceive it. In a dream, in a vision of the night, when deep sleep falls upon men, while slumbering on their beds, then He opens the ears of men, and seals their instruction." Job 33:14-16*

Rebecca had been clean from drugs for less than a year. The following morning, she told the group how she had been dreaming someone was trying to get her to take drugs again. Clearly the enemy was coming to her in her sleep. Suddenly, she heard someone yell, "Put that down right now!" Startled out of her sleep, Rebecca sat straight up in bed. She soon realized Fonda was talking in her sleep. The Spirit of God spoke these words emphatically through Fonda, loud enough to wake Rebecca from her bad dream. God intervened, revealing Himself while they were sleeping. Even while they were unconscious, He used Fonda's words to speak into her roommate's situation. The spirit of God transcends time, space, and sleep. We need to remember that God is limitless, eternal, and always present. He is almighty and all knowing. His ways are higher than our own.

Spirit of Prophecy

"And Jesus said to them, "I am the bread of life. He who comes to Me shall never hunger, and he who believes in Me shall never thirst." John 6:35

When we arrived in Shasta, we had barely emptied the car and settled in when the women gathered around a table with Bibles and notebooks in hand. They were so eager and hungry to meet with God. He was just as eager to meet with us. He satisfied the very longings of our hearts as He revealed Himself intimately and powerfully.

Carol, a new friend at the Shasta getaway, was grieving. A week prior, she had lost a friend to cancer who was like a mother to her. Other circumstances hadn't turned out as she had dreamed. Blindsided by loss and disappointment, her heart was shattered. Her situation had robbed her joy.

We were having a ministry time praying specifically over each person. God showed me a picture of Carol standing under a massive waterfall. When I shared this, she immediately opened her eyes in unbelief and said, "That's exactly what I just saw." The Holy Spirit was right there with us, making Himself known again to one of His own who had lost her spark. God's love for Carol couldn't be contained or held back. He was showing her a waterfall that represented a baptism of His love. It washed over her with power and certainty.

Prophecy is simply hearing God's voice through the Holy Spirit. Most people assume since prophecy is listed as a gift of the Spirit, it's not something they've been given. All of us with the same Spirit of God dwelling in us have been given the ability to hear Him; some people have just developed it better than others.

I explained this to the women, and I don't think they fully believed me. To demonstrate what I was saying, I led them in a practice of hearing God's voice. Before we started, I went into my bedroom and got on my face before God. I prayed, "I really need You, and I'm trusting you to reveal Yourself to these women. Thank you for what you are getting ready to do."

> *"The Lord God has given me the tongue of the learned, that I should know how to speak, a word in season to him who is weary. He awakens Me morning by morning, he awakens My ear to hear as the learned." Isaiah 50:4*

The Spirit of prophecy is Jesus. Every prophet in the Bible was pointing to Him. Every prophetic word still given should somehow point to Him. The Spirit of God reveals Jesus. In the book of Revelation, the Holy Spirit came to John and gave him the ability to see Jesus for who He really is. Revelation is a book of the revelation of Jesus. Prophecy is simple then. What is the Spirit saying about Jesus? What is Jesus saying to us by His Spirit?

Activation:

We drew names as if we were drawing names for Christmas. I told them not to look at the name they had drawn. I didn't tell them we were practicing the prophetic. I told them to close their eyes and ask God for a word or picture. I said, "He might give more than one. Just write what you hear or see. There's no right or wrong answer. You don't have to be afraid." Once they were settled on the idea that this wasn't a test, they relaxed and listened for 5 to 10 minutes. The wind began to pick up. We could hear the sound of the wind chimes, and I could feel God's presence.

As we went around to share what God had given us, Fonda went first. She had three words. As she listed them, my friend Mary, looked at me confused. With a sense of childlikeness, she said, "She got my words."

I thought, "This is getting ready to be good." After Fonda listed her words, she opened the name she had drawn. It was Mary. Mary looked at me in disbelief. Because her name was the one Fonda had drawn she was next to share what God had given her. As she shared her words, she explained that she and Fonda had the same words. Mary said, "I know this wasn't me making this up, because I don't even use this word." She listed her three words then opened the name she had drawn. It was Fonda. Everyone's eyes were bulging at this point. They hugged and cried and hugged some more. We couldn't believe it. God had given two women the same words for each other. The session continued on and as we shared what God had given us, a similar thing happened with two other women. The second set of women experienced seeing pictures rather than hearing words. God was revealing Himself, confirming to these women that they were hearing and seeing Him.

Love is a person. Peace has a name. Jesus. I love that we get to bare all to Jesus. He already knows everything in our hearts and minds, but He invites us to come away into the deep to be transparent with Him. He wants to listen and hear what we have to say. It's where we lay ourselves out naked before Him. It's so much more than skin deep. It's real and raw, honest relationship. It is where we seek more of Him, not because we want something from Him. We desire to see Him face to face because we love Him. He reveals Himself. We hear Him and taste His goodness. Those who have ears let them hear what the Spirit says...

Prayer:

Holy Spirit, Thank You for being the Revealer of all truth, our Counselor and friend. Open our ears to hear you and eyes to see you. Make yourself clearly known to us. Guide us each and every day, giving us wisdom and direction that can only come from you. Help us mine out nuggets of truth from Your Word that we've never unearthed before. Use our mouths to speak forth the words of God. Help us to know how to live our lives in a way that pleases You and represents the love of our Father to the world. In Jesus name. Amen.

CHAPTER TEN

Facing The Wind

"Aim at heaven and you will get earth thrown in. Aim at earth and you get neither."
~ C.S. Lewis

WHEN I WAS A child, I received a kite as a gift. Higher and higher it flew, and my excitement escalated. My little heart pounded as my hands clenched around the string. Because we lived surrounded by trees, it wasn't long until my new kite was stuck in the top of a tree, never to return. Hot tears streamed down my face as my seven-year-old dreams of flying my kite to the clouds never came to pass.

After I was married and living in California, David and I ventured to the beach with a new kite. Northern California beaches are typically cool and windy. Dreams from my childhood came to pass as I flew our kite all over that empty beach. I'm easily entertained. It's the small things that make me smile. I was fascinated by how high the wind would take the kite with no effort from me. I watched it lift higher and higher. Resting on the wind, the kite did what it was created to do, soar!

When we rest on the wind of the Holy Spirit, He takes us higher. Inevitably out of our control, circumstances come our way to attempt to bring us down. Instead of striving to fix them, we can rest knowing God is in control. It could be easy to become confused and fearful by what we see with our natural eyes. When we seek God's perspective, He gives us wisdom and discernment to see beyond what most people can see. Those with their hearts fixed on things above will find themselves unhindered by the entanglements of human voices and worldly noise.

David praised God on the day he was delivered from Saul and all his enemies:

> *"He (God) bowed the heavens also, and came down with darkness under His feet. He rode upon a cherub, and flew; And He was seen upon the wings of the wind. He made darkness canopies around Him, Dark waters and thick clouds of the skies. From the brightness before Him coals of fire were kindled." 2 Samuel 22:10-13*

God rides upon the wings of the wind. When we're willing to fly with Him, we rise above earthly resistance to a dimension where we get to see from God's perspective.

Facing Resistance

Our direction is more important than our location. Some of us are directionally challenged. When we point ourselves in the right direction, we will reach our destination. Regardless of our location or the situation in which we find ourselves, we will fly when we lean into the wind of the Spirit of God. The resistance I've faced in writing this book has been substantial, but I've set my gaze on Jesus. Anytime we set out to do what God has asked us to do, there will be resistance, whether natural or spiritual. The enemy (Satan) does not want us to succeed at becoming who God created us to be. If he knew he could get by with it, rather than hinder us, he would destroy us.

That's just what he attempted to do with my friend, Judy. She and her husband had made plans to take their annual beach trip for a month in the fall. Due to a last minute, unexpected change in plans, her husband didn't go with her on the beginning of their trip. Judy traveled alone, which was devastating to her. Brokenhearted, she was left feeling isolated, rejected and abandoned. Satan is opportunistic and targeted her emotional wounds from the past to begin spoon-feeding her lies during her first few hours there. "Why are you here alone? This wasn't the way it was planned. You're always going to be alone. You're not enough. Your life doesn't matter. You're worthless. You're not loveable. Nobody cares. If they cared, they'd be here with you. Why don't you just take your life? You could just take those pills and no one would ever know. Just kill yourself."

Before Judy left that day, she had attended a class I was teaching on identity. Typically, I'm not a huge fan of handouts. However, at the last minute, just before teaching, the Lord nudged me to make copies of a list of key scriptures about who we are in Christ. When Judy arrived at the beach and began hearing those lies, God reminded her of the list in her Bible from that morning. She used it to speak and pray truth, which helped her overcome the trap of believing the lies. She worshipped God and declared who He is and who she is as His child.

A pivotal point was when she heard the enemy say, "Judy, just take the pills. Lay down, listen to the waves, and you'll go to sleep." When the enemy used those words in particular, he had crossed the line.

When she was a child, Judy and her family would often stay in a trailer in Canada near the beach. During their trips to the ocean, when Judy didn't want to go to bed, her mother would say, "Judy, lay down, listen to the waves, and you'll go to sleep." The very same words that had been a comfort to her in the past, the enemy was now using to try to destroy her. He wanted to convince her of how easy it would be to just take some pills and go to sleep.

She described her response: "I battled. I karate chopped. I yelled the truth of who I am back to the lies of the enemy. I went through the list of scriptures, over and over. This went on for most of the night. The battle was fierce. Finally, the voice grew silent. The Word of God was my weapon, and the Spirit of God came to my defense. He won!"

Since her parents had abandoned Judy, a key for her victory in this battle was that she knew, believed, spoke, and held on to who she is as God's child. Both of Judy's parents and a set of grandparents had taken their own lives through suicide. It was generational. Judy used the keys God had placed in her hands: the weapon of His Word, what Jesus had done on the cross, praising Him, and the truth of who she is as His daughter.

Paul and Silas knew what it was like to face resistance when they found themselves in prison.

> *"But at midnight Paul and Silas were praying and singing hymns to God, and the prisoners were listening to them. Suddenly there was a great earthquake, so that the foundations of the prison were shaken; and immediately all the doors were opened and everyone's chains were loosed." Acts 16:25-26*

Paul and Silas were immovable, unshaken by their situation. Rather than being moved by our circumstances, may our circumstances be moved by us.

Much like what Judy did by praying and declaring the Word, Paul and Silas praised God in the midst of a terrible situation. The light of Jesus inside them lit up the darkness everywhere they found themselves. Being bound up in chains would have been earth shattering for most, but they faced it with joy, because they knew who they were and whose they were. Not long after they started singing, three things happened as a result of "a great earthquake." The foundation of the prison was shaken, doors were opened, and chains were loosed. FREEDOM!

The foundations were shaken. Most of us know the enemy doesn't work overnight. He works over a lifetime, scheming to take us to one grand pivotal moment where he tries to finally take us down. The enemy does his best to create a foundation of wounds: words spoken, acts done against us, lies we've believed about others and ourselves. Because of what Judy had experienced, she may have believed that she wasn't good enough for her mom and dad to even want to live. Or, maybe she believed those closest to her would always leave her alone. These lies were planted when she was young, after her parents left her. The enemy builds on painful experiences. But the Word says, the foundations were shaken. If we praise our way through the rough times, God will shake the very foundations of the prison.

Doors opened, making an easy way of escape. There was a way for the prisoners to get out. Judy had that list in her Bible. It was an easy access, open door for her. God had put that in her possession so she would have a quick tool to use to pray and declare the truth of her identity.

God doesn't stop there. Chains were loosed. He doesn't want us out of prison and still bound by the chains. God desires for us to have full freedom. And that is just what He did for Judy. She is now busy using her gifts, helping with a local ministry. She's a fiercely strong, world-changing woman of God. The enemy wanted to take her out before she fully knew who she was and the authority she had. But God gave her just what she needed for that battle and rescued her with truth. Through the battle, she found out who she really is because she realized to Whom she belongs. Instead of being moved by the deception and intensity of her circumstance, she kept her eyes fixed upward, head turned facing the wind, and she was loosed to fly.

When we look to the Holy Spirit to guide us and face our fears and difficulties with His help, we rise above the resistance. When we get high enough, we can finally rest and see things a little clearer. His power fuels us upward and gives us the perseverance to keep on when everything in us wants to quit. Just like eagles take the higher way when they spread their wings and face the wind, we fly higher when we face Jesus.

"Delight yourself in the Lord; and I (He) will cause you to ride on the high hills of the earth." Isaiah 58:14

A Bird's-Eye View

"Who may ascend into the hill of the Lord? Or who may stand in His holy place? He who has clean hands and a pure heart." Psalm 24:3-4

God brought Carole Ann and me together as the closest of friends more than ten years ago. He has preserved our friendship through many ups and downs. We've been appointed by God to minister together just as He called the disciples to go "two by two" to preach the gospel, heal the sick, and set the captives free. The purpose of

Him sending the two of us is much the same.

Last February, Carole Ann and I ministered at a women's retreat in the mountains of North Carolina. Normally we are pretty worn out after intense ministry times. This particular time was no different, so after that retreat, we ventured out for a mountain getaway of our own. The area hotels had limited availability, so we drove to another little town I had never visited. It was late in the evening when we started, so we crossed the mountain in the dark and fog.

The hotel we found was historic. As we stood in line to check in, a newspaper article was framed on the wall with headlines saying the hotel was haunted. Neither of us needs any help with our imaginations. We both read the article with our eyes bulging and looked at one another. Since it was so late we decided we would stay, "haunted" or not. While she was in the bathroom washing her face, I was doing some cleaning of my own. I was spiritually house cleaning that room with prayer. I was not spending the night with any spirits except the Holy Spirit. We slept like peaceful babies.

The next day was beautiful and the place looked entirely different. In daylight, it was much more inviting. We found a cute restaurant that served only fresh, organic foods. After eating, God led us to a place to hike. I didn't realize what we were getting ourselves into. When I say hike, I mean it. We must have climbed a mile straight up. The hike was gorgeous, with lookouts along the way. It was as if God was speaking to us through the hike. I could see symbolism of my journey with Him literally spelled out, written as the names of the overlooks. We went through a cave-like tunnel. What seemed difficult turned out to be a shortcut. We climbed the stairs, up and up. At one point we were between two huge mountains of rock. We couldn't see anything on either side. There was no view of where we were headed or where we had been. Most of us have certainly felt that way at times on our journey with God. Sometimes it's difficult to remember all that He's brought us through and we have no idea where we're headed next.

We reached what I thought was the top as we came to the rock with the American flag waving in the wind. Success! We made it. Carole Ann decided we needed to keep climbing. She wanted to know where we would end up if we went right instead of left to the flag. Up we continued. We came to several lookouts as we climbed. It was incredible how God pointed out my life's journey with Him on this mountain. The names of the lookouts, in the order we came to them were the pulpit, the opera overlook, devil's head, and exclamation point.

The Pulpit: I grew up in traditional church. My life was full of experiences with church and pulpits. I was saved at an early age. Of course, growing up in the church shaped my story.

Opera Overlook: I initially pursued music before deciding to become a nurse. I was a voice major and sang in operas, which is almost comical to me now. Though I have an appreciation for opera, I can't imagine dedicating myself to it. Music remains one of my loves, but I'm more inspired by worship now.

Devil's Head: After I was married with small children, I started believing lies about my marriage, about God, about the church. For a short period I rebelled against all of it. I could have lost my marriage and everything precious in my life, but God is faithful. He pulled me out of it, forgave me and set me free from shame. I had been singing "Jesus Loves Me" my whole life, but it was through that season that I learned experientially about God's love. I also discovered what a liar Satan is and how he wants to destroy us. This wasn't something I had been taught in my years as a child in Sunday school. Out of necessity, I learned about spiritual warfare and how to take the "devil's head" in prayer. I quickly learned about the schemes of the enemy and how to overcome. We have authority through the Word of God and the blood and name of Jesus.

As we moved closer to the top of the mountain, the trails were a little bit less refined. Earlier there had been stairs built in the side of the mountain, but now the trail was rugged. We were hiking on rocks and narrow, bumpy paths. Isn't that the way it is when we are ascending the hill of the Lord? It's not easy but so worth it.

Exclamation Point: There, we had a panoramic view where we could see for miles. God took us up to get a bird's-eye view. It was a place of intimacy with Him, so quiet you could hear Him whisper. We could feel the wind in our faces. It was a view from where He sits, high above the noise. It was picturesque of my life in the past couple of years. I've been in a place of intimacy with Him, a secret, hidden place where I have been still and listening. It's been a time of receiving and allowing Him to change my mind about who He is and who I am. I've had the time of my life in this place and wouldn't trade it for anything.

As we were on our way back down, we passed all of those places again. God spoke to us from a different perspective when we were going down. The Lord orders our steps, and our hike was a prophetic picture of where we've been and where we're headed.

We finally stopped on our way down at the lookout with the American flag. My heart is for America. God loves this country. He wants us free from our divisions and ourselves. From sea to shining sea, He wants us to stand united as brothers and sisters under Him. I believe that day is just ahead. We are one nation, under God, indivisible, with liberty and justice for all. America, God shed His grace on thee.

Carole Ann and I climbed that mountain and the Lord showed us His perspective. He took us up where the eagles soar. Gladys Aylward, a British missionary to China, once said, "The eagle that soars in the upper air does not worry itself how it is to cross rivers." When we get God's perspective, we don't have to fear the obstacles and entanglements of the world. God was teaching us the most beautiful place is up, with Him. The higher way is the best way, His way.

> "As the heavens are higher than the earth, so are my ways higher than your ways and my thoughts than your thoughts." Isaiah 55:9 (NIV)

A Spacious Place

> "At the blast of the breath of His nostrils. He (God) sent from above, He took me, He drew me out of many waters. He delivered me from my strong enemy, From those who hated me; For they were too strong for me. They confronted me in the day of my calamity, But the LORD was my support. He also brought me out into a broad place; He delivered me because He delighted in me." 2 Samuel 22:16b-19

God breathes on our situation from above. He draws us up and out, away from our enemies. We get to soar above the resistance by the might and power of His Spirit. He's our rescue and will set our feet in spacious places of deliverance from all that may try to hold us back.

As I mentioned before, I have a story of going away from God. The beautiful thing is that He never went away from me. As long as I live, I'll never forget the night He wooed me back. In that season, I had questioned Him. I had been in a dry spiritual time when I felt distant from God. I began to doubt and question Him. After associating Him with the weaknesses of religion and the church, I ran from God for several months.

While I was in that place of rebellion, one particular night He made Himself known to me. I was in a place of shame, but I could feel His presence so tangibly. It was as if another human was standing in the room with me, breathing. His presence was heavy. I knew it was undeniably Him. Feeling such conviction over where I'd been, I said, "Please don't look at me God. Please don't." But, He had already seen it all.

That's when He began to tell me how much He loved me. I knew if I kept going in the direction I had previously been headed, I was doomed for destruction. That night was a turning point because I felt Him loving me back. I had always thought I knew about His love, but in that moment I encountered it firsthand. He still loved me through my mess. He chose to forgive and forget, just as if it had never happened. I experienced His love for me like never before in that moment. I'm still brought to tears at the thought of how He saved me. He pulled me up and out of my situation. He set my feet high on a rock.

"He also brought me up out of a horrible pit, out of the miry clay, and set my feet upon a rock, and established my steps."
Psalm 40:2

Before I knew any of God's plans for me and while I was still in a rebellious season, He moved me all the way to my home in North Carolina. He literally removed me from my situation. Not only that, He positioned me to fulfill His plans for my life before I even knew there was a plan. God blessed my husband and me more monetarily than we ever dreamed possible. He even gave us land in the countryside of North Carolina, which had always been a dream of mine. Like King David, He set my feet in a spacious place, because He delighted in me. He didn't delight in what I was doing at the time. He didn't delight in the sin in my life, but He loved who He had created me to be. God is all knowing, and He delighted in who He knew I would become. When I least deserved it, He brought me into a spacious place. I understand, we never deserve what He's done for us, but He chooses to do it anyway. Every day I'm in awe of the faithfulness and goodness of God.

May we begin to see people through God's eyes, regardless of where they are or who they are right now. From His perspective, they are worth delighting in. They are worth knowing the truth of His love for them! They are worth a spacious place where they can be set free to soar! May we see beyond who people are to who they will become. It's important that we begin seeing others and ourselves as forgivable, lovable, and worth pursuing—the way God sees us. We are created in His image. Fearfully and wonderfully made, we are extremely valuable to God. He does not make mistakes, so we should love and treat one another (and ourselves) with dignity and respect.

God's might is seen by what He does through the weak! Out of our adversity comes greatness. Ask the Holy Spirit to help you see from His perspective. Make a choice to look on things above, which are unseen and eternal. As we gaze upon the face of Jesus in our weaknesses, we are given Spirit-breathed supernatural ability to fly. What we thought was impossible is suddenly within reach.

Prayer:
Jesus, Oh how we love you. Take us up on a mountain high. Give us your perspective. As resistance comes and we choose to look to you, take us up higher to see from your perspective. Thank you, God, that your ways are higher than our ways and your thoughts higher than our thoughts. Your word and will in heaven is flawless. We call it forth and trust it in our own lives, even when we don't fully understand it. We know you are trustworthy, so we choose to trust you, God. We choose today to take a deep breath, spread our arms out wide, open our hands, and look up. We choose to soar. In Jesus' name. Amen!

CHAPTER ELEVEN

Sound Of Rain

*"And make preparation: for already the
wind rises, the leaves rustle in the trees;
the birds hasten to their nests, and lo I
come. I come to revive and to refresh. I
come to quicken and cleanse. I come as
floods upon parched ground."*
~ *Frances J. Roberts*

I GREW UP IN North Carolina. As a child, I don't recall having droughts. However, as an adult I have seen them here on occasion. Recently, we had such a severe drought, it lasted into fall and winter. Fires popped up all over the state, some worse than California wildfires. I'm reminded of a vision I had while praying on a conference call with some North Carolina leaders. During our prayer time, I saw an aerial view of North Carolina, as one would see from an airplane. It appeared dark, and I saw the shape of the state as outlined on a map with pockets of fire scattered across the state.

When God shows us something in a vision or dream, we shouldn't be afraid. The best response is to pray. Take it into the courts of heaven. Let God be the judge. He often will show us things so we know how to pray.

At that time, North Carolina had been in the news as we had taken a difficult stand on some controversial issues. Everyone in America had been watching, some in disdain and others in admiration. In the vision, I was sure God was saying we were creating a significant light in the United States, like a city on a hill that couldn't be hidden. It was a picture of what was to come in the Spirit. Fire was representing God's Spirit and revival bursting forth all across the state. I never dreamed we would have literal fires in the natural.

God will occasionally show us things in the natural to reveal what is happening, or what is to come, in the Spirit. I'm still believing for the promise of spiritual revival and awakening in North Carolina and across the United States. I believe for the promise of the fire of the Spirit of God to sweep across the land and consume everything in its path.

When I heard of these actual fires, I prayed, "Lord, send Your rain, literally." But I sensed these fires were somehow a display of the glory of God. I have to agree with Billy Graham, who once said, "In an age that is given over to cynicism, coldness, and doubt and in which the fire and warmth of God is conspicuous for its absence in the world, my heart cry is, let the fire fall. Oh, God, let the fire of your love fall on us."

I am reminded of Elijah, an Old Testament prophet, who lived in a time of extreme drought, poverty, corrupt governmental leadership, false prophets, and idol worship. He was not a prophet who tickled the ears of the people or stayed within the four walls of the temple. He called out the evil leaders, false prophets and their idolatry. He stood for truth and found himself often isolated. Typically, signs and wonders followed him. Elijah heard God, followed Him, and believed Him to do the impossible.

Today, we are living in a time of uncertainty, lawlessness, spiritual drought, and idol worship. But, we are going to see a revival in this generation such as has never been seen on the earth. We are not going to just hear messages about God; we are going to see Him reveal Himself in power. We are called to be men and women, like Elijah, who believe God and follow through with what He's saying. Where we go, signs and wonders will follow because the Spirit of God is alive in us. As with Elijah (1 Kings 18:1), God's children will listen to the voice of the LORD, obey, pray, and trust God to fulfill what He speaks. We will count on God, and He will perform the miraculous.

Drought

Five or six years ago, we were having a worship party behind my house. For a week prior, the forecast called for rain. I sat in my office that morning and prayed. "Lord, You are the same God who parted the Red Sea. I know I'm asking for something simple for You. Please hold back the clouds. Part the sky over this field like you parted the Red Sea. Hold the rain back from this bonfire. Let Your glory be revealed to everyone here by answering this prayer, in Jesus' name. Amen." Right then, I opened my Bible and it fell open to James 5:17.

> *"Elijah was a human being, even as we are. He prayed earnestly that it would not rain, and it did not rain on the land for three and a half years." James 5:17 (NIV)*

I knew then it would not rain. People mentioned the 100 percent chance of rain forecast all day. The party was underway. Still no rain. My friend Laurie was driving in from out of town, trying to get to the party. She called and said, "There's no way we can get there. The weather is just too bad." She asked how our weather was, and I told her it was clear above us but looked stormy in the distance and all around us. She said she could see a clear spot in our location but all around us was red and green on her phone's Doppler radar.

In His great glory, God held the clouds and rain back and opened the sky's canopy over our heads. We worshiped under the stars in the middle of a major storm. King Ahab worshiped Baal, the god of rain. To prove who was really in control of the weather, Elijah said to Ahab:

> *"As the Lord God of Israel lives, before whom I stand, there shall not be dew nor rain these years, except at my word."* 1 Kings 17:1

Elijah used his God-given authority and spoke with confidence. He delivered God's message and God delivered the results. It takes courage to step out with this kind of boldness, but God is so much bigger than what we can see with earthly eyes.

During this more than three year drought, Elijah followed every move the Lord told Him to make. His life depended on it. God told Him to go and hide near a brook, and He commanded the ravens to feed him there. When the brook dried up, God sent him to a widow with only enough flour and oil to feed herself and her son one last time. Elijah told her if she would make a portion for him first, the flour and oil would never run out.

This was such a beautiful kingdom picture. Give to God or to those who belong to Him first, and our provisions will never run dry. Follow His lead every step of the way, and we will never lack anything. This is so contrary to the world's systems and mindset. She did what was asked of her and sure enough, she always had plenty to feed all three of them. What a miracle of provision! I've read similar stories of provision from Heidi Baker, a missionary to Mozambique, Africa. Like the fishes and the loaves or this miracle of Elijah's provision, she and her husband have often offered what little they had and fed hundreds of orphans then had leftovers remaining.

Sometimes we feel like we have nothing left, nothing to offer, or the little we have to give isn't much. We may be in a drought ourselves and in need of heavenly provision. Bring the little you have, and He will multiply it with the oil of His presence. Miracles follow faith and obedience, not pomp and circumstance. If we will trust God and act out of pure love and obedience rather than out of human reasoning, we will see more than we ever dreamed possible this side of heaven.

During the drought, Elijah saw some of the biggest miracles of his life. Elijah was fed by ravens and sent to multiply a widow's food. God directed Elijah to be in the right place at the right time. While he was staying with this widow and her son, the boy became ill to the point of death.

> *"And his sickness was so serious that there was no breath left in him." 1 Kings 17:17b*

Elijah went to the boy and cried out to God:

> *"'O Lord my God, have You also brought tragedy on the widow with whom I lodge, by killing her son?' And he stretched himself out on the child three times, and cried out to the Lord and said, 'O Lord my God, I pray, let this child's soul come back to him.' Then the Lord heard the voice of Elijah; and the soul of the child came back to him, and he revived. And Elijah took the child and brought him down from the upper room into the house, and gave him to his mother." 1 Kings 17:20-24*

During one of Elijah's most difficult seasons, he saw God's faithfulness as He restored life to the widow's son.

"And Elijah said, 'See, your son lives!' Then the woman said to Elijah, 'Now by this I know that you are a man of God, and that the word of the Lord in your mouth is the truth.'" (verse 24)

The widow confessed she believed him to be a prophet. Isn't it interesting how we often don't believe the truth people speak to us about God. We have to see it or hear it for ourselves. Some people don't believe God until He reveals Himself through the miracle. Faith believes for the miracle of rain in the drought. In the rough times, when we feel like we might die, we're given supernatural opportunities to trust, follow, and rest. In the most difficult seasons of our lives, it is helpful to remember that God has not changed. If we focus on God, who is able to do far more than we can imagine, we will stand firm. If we focus on our feelings or circumstances, we are likely to waiver. His ability to heal, resurrect, and provide never changes or runs out.

Under the Broom Tree

While preparing to write this chapter, I was blindsided by feelings of fear, anxiety, loneliness, isolation, and wanting to quit. I was a mess. This was so unlike me. I'm not normally afraid, especially to speak truth, nor do I fight feelings of loneliness. I actually enjoy time alone with God, but this particular evening, I was overwhelmed with feelings of loneliness and fear. Admittedly, I had been isolated more than usual while writing. Still, these thoughts were sudden and unexpected.

I knew this was a spiritual battle. A tearful mess, I prayed. Declaring truth, I knew God was with me. Fear of man overwhelmed. People don't typically want to read about being set apart to God. Most don't want to hear about repentance and obedience. These are just not popular subjects. Fear of rejection taunted. I worshipped, thanking God. I repented of anything in me that shouldn't be, like fearing what people think more than what He thinks. I asked God to forgive me for not trusting Him in this. I read the Word. No matter what, these feelings were unrelenting. I was shaken to my core. Finally, I called and talked to a friend who spoke truth and prayed me through.

During this entire event, God was delivering, healing and preparing me on deeper levels. It was a breakthrough of sorts. He was taking me to new heights of His glory. I was going up, but it didn't feel like it. Actually the opposite felt true. By the end of the night, I felt something release. I knew I had come through something, almost like birthing.

God showed me in my struggle that Elijah had many of the same feelings. He had been battling it out with Jezebel and Ahab by calling all of their prophets of Baal and the people of Israel to Mt Carmel. Elijah brought them together and asked,

> *"How long will you falter between two opinions? If the Lord is God, follow Him; but if Baal, follow him." 1 Kings 18:21*

Empowered by God, this was fierce and bold. Elijah had to be unaffected by the opinions of men. Elijah asked for two bulls. He instructed Baal's prophets to choose their bull, cut it up, and place it on the wood, but put no fire under it. Elijah said he would do the same with the other bull. He told them to pray to their god and he would pray to his. The one who responded with fire was the True God. Baal's prophets prayed and their idol didn't respond. Elijah prayed, and God consumed the entire altar with fire. This was a mighty display of God's glory. Then Elijah executed all the false prophets.

Once evil Queen Jezebel heard what had happened, she threatened to kill Elijah. He had to run and hide for his life.

> *"But he himself went a day's journey into the wilderness, and came and sat down under a broom tree. And he prayed that he might die, and said, 'It is enough! Now, Lord, take my life, for I am no better than my fathers!' Then as he lay and slept under a broom tree, suddenly an angel touched him, and said to him, 'Arise and eat.'" 1 Kings 19:4-5*

Elijah was one of the most powerful God-anointed men to ever walk the earth. But his life was challenging and difficult. He was a mighty man, called to great exploits on the earth. But after this miraculous victory, Elijah ran in fear. He was depressed and hiding from Queen Jezebel.

Surrounding our most monumental successes or breakthroughs, we experience the fiercest battles. I've seen this multiple times when I've spoken to large groups. If you've ever tried to do anything big for God, there has most definitely been spiritual resistance.

Before or after, there are typically thoughts of wanting to quit. Feelings of oppression and anxiety try to overpower rational thoughts. For me, quitting isn't an option. Quitting is not God's will for us, especially if He's asked us to do something, but sometimes it feels like a reasonable response. That's exactly what the enemy would like for us to do. Quit. That is even more of a reason to pray and persevere through.

> *"For though we walk in the flesh, we do not war according to the flesh. For the weapons of our warfare are not carnal but mighty in God for pulling down strongholds, casting down arguments and every high thing that exalts itself against the knowledge of God, bringing every thought into captivity to the obedience of*

Christ, and being ready to punish all disobedience when your obedience is fulfilled." 2 Corinthians 10:3-6

When we are under attack, one of our best defenses is first identifying the spirit we are battling. In Revelation, John wrote what God said to the church in Thyatira. He warned them of being seduced by Jezebel. He was referring to a spirit, not the actual person. The spirit of Jezebel is contrary to the spirit of Elijah. This nasty spirit will do everything possible to silence the man or woman of God: causing fear, isolation, depression, and immobilization. The goal is ultimately the same as Satan's goal of destruction and death. However, if the spirit of Jezebel can stop the people of God from doing what they've been called to do, that will suffice.

That is exactly what was happening with Elijah under the broom tree. He had battled it out. He had dismantled the power of the enemy by killing false prophets. Jezebel knew she was next. Elijah was hiding from Jezebel, because she wanted to see him dead. When we find ourselves under the broom tree, weary and worn from the battle, remember the Lord is faithful. Elijah was awakened to a little angel food cake and some water. God sent His angelic messenger and provisions.

When we are feeling afraid, weary, inadequate for the task, or alone, God sees. Under the broom tree of battle and feelings of defeat, God sees. Ask God to identify the evil spirit at work, and then take authority over it in Jesus' name. The spirit of depression, deceit, death, lust, or whatever it might be, command it to leave in Jesus' name, and it will flee.

"Therefore submit to God. Resist the devil and he will flee from you. Draw near to God and He will draw near to you. Cleanse your hands, you sinners; and purify your hearts, you double-

153

minded. *Lament and mourn and weep! Let your laughter be turned to mourning and your joy to gloom. Humble yourselves in the sight of the Lord, and He will lift you up." James 4:7-10*

Rain

While living in California for the first nine years of my marriage, I missed the rain. California is known for its mild weather and sunshine. Though I loved the dry weather, this Southern girl missed the sound of summer thunderstorms and occasionally sleeping with the rain hitting the roof. Something about rain is cozy, secure, and comforting. I know the earth appreciates it, like taking a big drink of refreshingly cold water on a hot day. I recall some funerals when God sent His rain, and it felt as though heaven was crying with me. Something about God seeing us in our weakness is comforting.

Israel hadn't seen rain for three and a half years because of idol worship. God told Elijah if he would go confront King Ahab, He would cause it to rain again. So Elijah did what was asked of him. That's when he told Ahab to gather all of Israel together at Mt. Carmel, and God consumed Elijah's altar with fire. Then, all the false prophets were executed.

> *"Then Elijah said to Ahab, 'Go up, eat and drink; for there is the sound of abundance of rain.'" 1 Kings 18:41*

Elijah went to the top of the mountain and bowed down with his face between his knees. He sent his servant seven times to look for a cloud over the sea. The seventh time he came back and reported:

> *"There is a cloud, as small as a man's hand, rising out of the sea!" (verse 44)*

Elijah was so confident in God's promise that he knew the small cloud meant rain was coming. He sent his messenger to tell Ahab.

> "*'Prepare your chariot, and go down before the rain stops you.'*
> *Now it happened in the meantime that the sky became black*
> *with clouds and wind, and there was a heavy rain."* (verses 44-
> 45)

Some of us have grown weary in the waiting. We know God has promised to do great things through us and for us. We are inside His storyline. I'm in the seventh year of waiting to see the fulfillment of some of God's promises in my life. I still believe. So, I encourage you—don't grow weary. Believe it before you see the slightest evidence of the promise, like Elijah. Keep praying and keep looking. Revival in the land is possible, even when we hear of, see, and experience drought, fire, famine, riots, fear, and uncertainty. I see a tiny cloud in the distance. Hitch up your chariots. Don't leave without your umbrellas. I hear the sound of the abundance of rain.

Prayer:
Father, Thank you that when there seems to be no way, when all seems lost, desperate, and dead, by faith we can trust Your promises. Thank you that no weapon of the enemy can stand against us. Jesus, you are our victory, and we choose to stand in the victory you've so generously given us. Today we choose to call forth the promises of God in our lives. We thank you for the sound of the abundance of rain. Pour out your blessings over your people. We receive it. In Jesus' name.

CHAPTER TWELVE

Royal Priests

"Every man gives his life for what he
believes. Every woman gives her life for
what she believes. Sometimes people
believe in little or nothing: One life is all
we have, and we live it as we believe in
living it, and then it's gone. But to
surrender what you are, and live without
belief—that's more terrible than dying—
more terrible than dying young."
~ Joan of Arc

DURING ONE OF MY adventures with a group of women to Moravian Falls, North Carolina, a woman who struggled with being open to things of the Spirit had a vision during the evening session. Uncertain and afraid, she didn't say anything about her vision that night. The next day, at the end of our time together, God had me share a word with these women about being queen priests.

"But you are a chosen people, a royal priesthood, a holy nation,

God's special possession, that you may declare the praises of him who called you out of darkness into his wonderful light." 1 Peter 2:9 (NIV)

God wants us to understand our role as royalty and as priests on the earth. I went around the room and extended my hand over each one's head like extending a royal scepter. God led me to commission them to go with confidence and do whatever He had called them to do. After this commissioning, the woman who had the vision the night before shyly spoke up, "You know this isn't like me. I don't have visions, but last night I saw Jesus going around the room touching each of us on our heads. That's what you just did. I couldn't believe my eyes as you went around to each one the way He did." To me, this was just confirmation that God had wanted me to commission these women to go.

We have been commissioned as queen (and king) priests to hear the word and will of the Lord. As priests we are to intercede or pray on others' behalf, and as royalty we've been positioned to make declarations of what we've heard from God. In doing so, we will see the GLORY of the Lord.

"And they sang a new song [of glorious redemption], saying, 'Worthy and deserving are You to take the scroll and to break its seals; for You were slain (sacrificed), and with Your blood You purchased people for God from every tribe and language and people and nation. You have made them to be a kingdom [of royal subjects] and priests to our God; and they will reign on the earth.'" Revelation 5:9-10 (AMP)

Prepare the Way

Before John the Baptist was born, an angel of the Lord came to John's father, Zacharias. The angel told him his wife would give him a son.

> *"For he will be great in the sight of the Lord, and shall drink neither wine nor strong drink. He will also be filled with the Holy Spirit, even from his mother's womb. And he will turn many of the children of Israel to the Lord their God. He will also go before Him (Jesus) in the spirit and power of Elijah, 'to turn the hearts of the fathers to the children, and the disobedient to the wisdom of the just, to make ready a people prepared for the Lord.'"* Luke 1:15-17

John would go before Jesus getting the people ready. He would call them to get their hearts right with God and right with one another. Jesus confirmed John the Baptist's role on earth when He said:

> *"For all the prophets and the law prophesied until John. And if you are willing to receive it, he is Elijah who is to come."* Matthew 11:13-14

Jesus also referred to this when he answered His disciples and said:

> *"'Indeed, Elijah is coming first and will restore all things. But I say to you that Elijah has come already, and they did not know him but did to him whatever they wished....' Then the disciples understood that He spoke to them of John the Baptist."* Matthew 17:11-13

Similar to Elijah, John the Baptist didn't tolerate religion. He was an outdoorsman who called people to repent and turn away from their sin. He was sent to prepare the way of the Lord. He went before Jesus to prepare the way for His teaching, miracles, and time on earth. Jesus said concerning John the Baptist:

"For this is he of whom it is written: "Behold, I send My messenger before Your face, who will prepare Your way before You." Matthew 11:10

John was in a position to call people to a life of obedience. He prepared those of his generation for the coming of Jesus Christ, the One who had come to seek and save the lost, and establish true reconciliation of people to their Father.

"Now all things are of God, who has reconciled us to himself through Jesus Christ, and has given us the ministry of reconciliation, that is, that God was in Christ reconciling the world to himself, not imputing their trespasses to them, and has committed to us the word of reconciliation. Now then, we are ambassadors for Christ, as though God were pleading through us: we implore you on Christ's behalf, be reconciled to God." 2 Corinthians 5:18-20

We each have a ministry of reconciliation. If we've been saved, we've been called. We have the privilege of being the messengers of hope to this generation. Francis Schaeffer said, "Each generation of the church in each setting has the responsibility of communicating the gospel in understandable terms, considering the language and thought-forms of that setting." Like John the Baptist and Elijah, we are sent ones to ready the Bride for Jesus' second coming. We are to tell the world about Jesus. The prophet Malachi prophesied of the "Elijah" who would return and prepare the way of the second coming of Jesus.

"See, I will send you the prophet Elijah before that great and dreadful day of the Lord comes. He will turn the hearts of the fathers to their children, and the hearts of the children to their fathers; or else I will come and strike the land with a curse." Malachi 4:5-6

Many people are waiting for Elijah's actual return. Just as John the

Baptist came in the spirit of Elijah, this generation is the fulfillment of Malachi's word concerning the return of Elijah. Our purpose is to "turn the hearts" of people, to see families restored, and prepare them for the Lord's second coming, thus the great and dreadful day of the Lord. This day will be dreadful for many, because He's coming to judge. People, get ready and make way for the King of glory, the One to whom all other kings and every person on earth will bow.

"This is Jacob, the generation of those who seek Him, Who seek Your face. Lift up your heads, O you gates! And be lifted up, you everlasting doors! And the King of glory shall come in. Who is this King of glory? The Lord strong and mighty, The Lord mighty in battle." Psalm 24:6-8

His Temple

Referring to the temple of His body, Jesus spoke. He knew He was going to die on the cross and be raised to life on the third day.

"Jesus answered them, 'Destroy this temple, and I will raise it again in three days.'" John 2:19 (NIV)

"We heard Him say, 'I will destroy this man-made temple, and in three days I will build another that is made without hands.'" Mark 14:58

Speaking of temples, Jesus not only was referring to His body as a temple that would be raised, but also our bodies are now temples. We get to host the presence of God everyday, everywhere we step our feet. He is dwelling with us. We house the Spirit of God.

"Do you not know that your bodies are members of Christ himself? ...Flee from sexual immorality. All other sins a person commits are

161

outside the body, but whoever sins sexually, sins against their own body. Do you not know that your bodies are temples of the Holy Spirit, who is in you, whom you have received from God? You are not your own; you were bought at a price. Therefore honor God with your bodies." 1 Corinthians 6:14-20 (NIV)

In the Old Testament, the tabernacle of God was a tent that could be moved from place to place. The Jews would follow God. They would see His presence in a cloud and they would know where to move the temple next. If we know Jesus personally, we are members of His Body making up a collective temple. He is the chief cornerstone of this building. We are God's house. He can't be contained in four walls, so He chooses to dwell with us through the Holy Spirit. Jesus was saying (as a human), He was the house of God and His house (temple) would be raised after three days. He's the Resurrection and the Life, who raises the dead to life. We are also raised in new life as we receive Him as Savior and have the Spirit dwelling inside us.

House Cleaning

A few years ago, I was planning a time at my parent's beach house with my friends, Mary and Maureen, from California. After hours of driving, I opened the door and was greeted by the most horrid odor I had ever smelled, a pretty bold statement coming from someone who has been a mom and a nurse. I went through the standard routines of turning all the breakers on, so I could see and hopefully figure out where that smell was coming from. As I opened the refrigerator to empty my travel cooler, I discovered the culprit. The last visitors to the house had accidentally flipped the breaker and turned the refrigerator off. It had been brewing in the heat for more than three weeks. The freezer was full of decaying meat.

162

I cleaned for hours. I went to bed at 2 a.m., woke up at 6 a.m. and cleaned again. The smell wasn't budging, so I mixed pure bleach with hot water and poured it through all the vents and lines in the refrigerator. Finally, something was helping. Bleach was a miracle worker.

Needless to say, the day I had planned to be a day of rest and relaxation with God wasn't possible. I tugged and pulled on huge bags of trash, dumping the contents of the refrigerator into a large trash can. I scrubbed, shop-vacuumed, hosed, bleached, and bought air fresheners. The refrigerator was very clean, but that smell was going to take some time to dissipate.

With only a couple of hours before my friends arrived, I had a conversation with God. I was so frustrated with the whole situation, not to mention I had hardly slept the night before from the stench. I asked, "Lord, what in the world is this all about? What are You trying to teach me here? I thought you wanted me to have a day alone with You!?!"

Immediately God spoke, "That's what your sin smells like to Me. When there's something in your life that you neglect to turn from and ask forgiveness for, that's how it smells to Me. It's decay in your life. And instead of giving off a sweet-smelling aroma, I smell the stench of your sin."

Obviously Jesus made a way for us to be forgiven, but repentance is a real and necessary thing. Repent comes from the Hebrew word, *shuwb*, meaning to turn back. So when we repent, we literally turn away from our sins and back to God. We turn around.

We all have rotting things hidden away in our soul closets, or in this case, refrigerators. Pride easily creeps in, or we idolize and worship the

Baals of materialism, entitlement, sectarianism, and legalism. We're no different than those Israelites. Consumed with self-pity and self-indulgence, we have taken the focus of our eyes and hearts off of the One who is worthy of worship and obedience. Routinely our hearts need a thorough Holy Spirit bleaching.

I recall the story of Naaman, the leper. A young Jewish servant girl had told Naaman's wife about Elisha: the prophet who was able to heal Naaman of his leprosy. Being an honorable man and commander of the army of the king of Syria, Naaman was granted permission from the king to go to Elisha, the prophet. Naaman was given specific directions about dipping in the Jordan River for his healing and cleansing. But, Naaman had expected something different. He was angry and didn't want to follow the instructions Elisha's messenger had given. Then one of Naaman's servants confronted him.

> *"My father, if the prophet had told you to do something great, would you not have done it? How much more then, when he says to you, 'Wash, and be clean'?" 2 Kings 5:13b*

Isn't this the truth? We want to do great things for God. Some want to lead revivals and preach to thousands, or lead great ministries that change the world. If we want to do great things, why is it so difficult to realize the importance of spiritual health and cleanliness before the Lord. Rick Warren says, "In ministry, private purity is the source of public power."

I've often said, what happens in private will be put on public display. In other words, what happens in secret (or doesn't happen) with God will be eventually evident on the platform. Most of us have great expectations of the way our future should unfold. God is merely asking us to be obedient. Similar to dipping in the river to be healed, sometimes His requests don't make sense and may even seem insignificant. He's looking at our hearts. He wants hearts and minds set apart and surrendered to Him, regardless of what He asks of us. God wants us to live in purity: clean lives dedicated to Him and what He is doing on the earth.

The priests of God were required to cleanse the inner parts of the temple.

> *"The priests went into the inner part of the house of the LORD to cleanse it, and they brought out all the uncleanness that they found in the temple of the LORD into the court of the house of the LORD. And the Levites took it and carried it out to the brook Kidron." 2 Chronicles 29:16 (KJV)*

Since we are God's children, the Holy Spirit dwells in us. Do we want Him to be comfortably at home in our inner being? If we desire to be clean and set apart for Him, we'll examine ourselves and invite Holy Spirit to show us what we need to see. God wants us to be honest with ourselves and ask, "Is what's in my heart representing the Holy Spirit? If not, Lord, show me, forgive me, and help me change it."

Turning hearts is something only the Holy Spirit can do. It's a message of repentance and reconciliation. God wants this message to be demonstrated in our own hearts before we ever speak it.

One of the most dangerous heart attitudes in the church is the one of Pharisees. Let us not forget the Pharisees were the religious leaders who knew the Word of God better than anyone. They were the experts in knowledge of the Word, yet they were caught up in traditions of men. They were condemning, judgmental, self-righteous, religious leaders who were more worried about whether people were eating clean or unclean than they were about the person's heart or healing. Jesus responded to their questioning.

"Hypocrites! Well did Isaiah prophesy about you, saying: 'These people draw near to Me with their mouth, And honor Me with their lips, But their heart is far from Me. And in vain they worship Me, Teaching as doctrines the commandments of men.'" Matthew 15:7-9

They quickly judged others and couldn't follow or believe Jesus due to the pride in their hearts. This has been a big problem in the church. This type of dishonoring behavior is legalism. It is having more concern for the law (lists of dos and don'ts) than the status of one's own heart. It's hypocrisy, or saying one thing but being and doing another. After referring to the Pharisees as hypocrites, Jesus said (to the multitude):

"'Hear and understand: Not what goes into the mouth defiles a man; but what comes out of the mouth, this defiles a man.'

Then His disciples came and said to Him,

'Do You know that the Pharisees were offended when they heard this saying?'

So Jesus said, 'Do you not yet understand that whatever enters the mouth goes into the stomach and is eliminated? But those things which proceed out of the mouth come from the heart, and they defile a man.'" Matthew 15:10-12, 17-18

Jesus had no tolerance for their hypocrisy. What is in our hearts truly matters to Him. Jesus is coming again to judge. He will judge what we have or haven't done with what He has given us: time, talent, spiritual gifts, etc. More than what we've done, our motives will be revealed. God cares about the motives of our hearts in our doing. He's not looking for our theology, religious offerings, or years devoted to our roots.

In Mark 11, Jesus overturned tables of moneychangers in the temple. He didn't like what He saw taking place inside the temple of God, so He let everyone there know it. Not only does Jesus want to shake things up and overturn the wrong tables in our individual hearts, He wants to shake up the church as we know it, the whole Body of believers.

"So don't turn a deaf ear to these gracious words. If those who ignored earthly warnings didn't get away with it, what will happen to us if we turn our backs on heavenly warnings? His voice that time shook the earth to its foundations; this time— he's told us this quite plainly—he'll also rock the heavens: "One last shaking, from top to bottom, stem to stern." The phrase "one last shaking" means a thorough housecleaning, getting rid of all the historical and religious junk so that the unshakable essentials stand clear and uncluttered. Do you see what we've got? An unshakable kingdom! And do you see how thankful we must be? Not only thankful, but brimming with worship, deeply reverent before God. For God is not an indifferent bystander. He's actively cleaning house, torching all that needs to burn, and he won't quit until it's all cleansed. God himself is Fire!"
Hebrews 12:26-29 (MSG)

Purifying our hearts may come in different forms and is necessary to be positioned and prepared by God to go. As royal priests we've been set apart to govern the house of God. We're being built into a house that can't be shaken, a house filled with his presence. We have been given keys to open and close doors in His kingdom. If we will take hold of love and use those keys in our spheres of influence, we will collectively change the world. Here are a few of the most valuable keys available to us:

Prayer:

Prayer is how we communicate with God. Through prayer, God is doing miracles behind the scenes. A life planted in prayer is the life that will produce great destiny. Prayer activates heaven, moves mountains, and shakes hell.

Humility:

Pride will mimic confidence, but there is a big difference between the two. Humble people are actually confident people because they are extremely aware of their God-identity. If humility truly is understanding who we are in relation to God, then knowing we're His can bring a great deal of relief and confidence—gentle, genuine, strong confidence. Where pride focuses on self, humility focuses on others.

Abbot Christopher Jamison said, "Humility is an honest approach to the reality of our own lives and acknowledges that we are not more important than other people."

> "Humble yourselves before the Lord, and he will lift you up."
> James 4:10 (NIV)

Pride is the opposite of humility and always manages to make everything about self. Pride generates quarrels (Proverbs 13:10), leads to self-dependence (1 Timothy 6:17), brings disgrace (Proverbs 11:2) and destruction (Proverbs 16:18), and it puts us in opposition to God (James 4:6). Pride is dangerous. Pride is why God kicked Satan out of heaven. God doesn't want us pridefully building our own kingdoms; He wants us building His. *"For yours is the kingdom, the power, and the glory forever."* It's not "mine is the kingdom." It all belongs to God, and to Him be all the glory forever.

In the kingdom, the way up is down. Zero gravity requires laying down at the foot of the cross. I've heard it said that humility is knowing who God is and who we are in relation to Him. Humility is often misunderstood as self-loathing or self-consciousness. These are actually false humility, which is pride. Humility is truly serving, complimenting, encouraging, and loving others without needing anything in return.

Surrender:

Open hands receive. We get to be gatekeepers not only for the house of our God, but also for our own houses, territories and spheres of influence. Willing hands do the work. Open hands can receive the keys.

Truth:

Priests are men and women of the Word. We are cleansed by the washing of water with the Word. David asked God how a young man could stay pure, then David answered his own question: by staying in the Word. Don't just read it; be transformed by it.

Purity:

> "He [David] So he shepherded them according to the integrity of
> his heart, And guided them by the skillfulness of his hands."
> Psalm 78:72

Purity is a matter of what's in the heart. Only God truly knows the extent and purity of our hearts. Today, sexual purity is difficult to maintain for many. Social media and increased access to electronic devices creates an open door to the enemy to try to tempt people. The likelihood of accidentally stumbling upon something sexual is higher today than ever. It is wise to be prepared for this and plan our responses in advance. God doesn't tempt us (James 1:13). We are lured by our own fleshly desires. So, when we are tempted, we must flee. Run. Get away from it. Pray.

Purity isn't whether or not we've ever sinned sexually but rather the status of our hearts right now with God. Once upon a time, my religious mind thought if I didn't have sex before marriage, I was pure. That was partially true, but I also needed to consider the purity of my mind. Purity isn't whether or not we've managed to keep our virginity before marriage. If we have sinned with our bodies, eyes or minds, we've sinned either way. Of course, God forgives, cleanses us, and makes us pure. But, He wants us to turn away from our sin, never to return to it. Purity isn't black and white and it's not a list of things to do or not do. It's the status of our hearts before God.

If you've struggled with an area of sexual purity, God can cleanse and set you free. He never wants us to live in a state of condemnation over past mistakes. He will wipe our slate clean and make us as pure as if it never happened. But He wants us surrendered to Him and not to our old habits. Purity is cleanness of thought, speech and conduct. Pray as David prayed:

> "Cleanse me from secret faults. Keep back Your servant also from presumptuous sins; Let them not have dominion over me. Then I shall be blameless, And I shall be innocent of great transgression. Let the words of my mouth and the meditation of my heart be acceptable in Your sight, O Lord, my strength and my Redeemer." Psalm 19:12b-14

After overturning some tables in our hearts, or cleansing us, Jesus redecorates and fills the inner chambers with even more of His Spirit. When Solomon built the temple of the Lord, the craftsmen who were masters of their trade built and carved all the furniture. Almost everything inside the temple was covered in gold. Inside the Holy of Holies, the most secret and Holy place of the temple, everything was covered in the finest gold. God is purifying our hearts through the fire, but in the end we will be inlaid with the purest gold—His presence.

"'Who of you is left who saw this house in its former glory? How does it look to you now? Does it not seem to you like nothing?...Be strong, all you people of the land,' declares the Lord, 'and work. For I am with you,' declares the Lord Almighty... 'And my Spirit remains among you. Do not fear...The glory of this present house will be greater than the glory of the former house,' says the Lord Almighty. 'And in this place I will grant peace,' declares the Lord Almighty." Haggai 2:3, 4b, 5b, 9 (NIV)

Refrigerator cleaning is a tough and grueling process, literally and spiritually. But when it's all over, the house is back to a sweet-smelling aroma. The glory of this present house will be greater than the glory of the former house. The former things will pass. We are made new in Christ. Our old mindset and ways of living must die before we can be resurrected to live in a new way. In Christ, our hearts and minds are made pure and clean before God.

Worship:
God isn't interested in our rituals and offerings, He's interested in the restoration of His family and messengers He can trust to speak the truth in love. God wants a generation unified and set apart for Him. Lives wholly, and holy, surrendered to Him is the worship He deserves and desires most. A nationwide or worldwide revival will never occur until revival occurs in the hearts of individual people. I often start messages on revival by having people hold their hand over their heart and say, "Revival starts here." Too often we become consumed with the idea and glamour of revival rather than being consumed by the ultimate revivalist, Jesus. Let us not worship revival but the One who revives. Let us not worship the healing or the experience we have but rather the One who heals or give us the experience. In His presence something within us shifts into right alignment every single time. He is and should forever be our ultimate focus. Encountering Jesus to the

point of inevitable change is revival.

> *"Indeed it came to pass, when the trumpeters and singers were as one, to make one sound to be heard in praising and thanking the Lord, and when they lifted up their voice with the trumpets and cymbals and instruments of music, and praised the Lord, saying: 'For He is good, For His mercy endures forever,' that the house, the house of the Lord, was filled with a cloud, so that the priests could not continue ministering because of the cloud; for the glory of the Lord filled the house of God." 2 Chronicles 5:13-14*

This house was filled with a cloud so that the priests could not continue. That's heavy! God's tangible presence could be felt and seen!! In times of unity in worship God is so pleased that He reveals Himself through His presence. He inhabits the praises of His people. The Father is particularly fond of us being one as He and Jesus are One. When praise and unity mesh an atmosphere is created for us to experience the fullness of God with no restraint. When this occurs, we get in on the party that has been continuously happening in heaven.

I'll never forget being in a stadium of believers in Los Angeles, California. More than 75,000 people were gathered in one place for one purpose. Jesus. As one voice, we worshipped the King of Kings. The tangible presence of God could be felt as it poured literal rain in this open stadium. The more we worshipped, the more it rained. Having lived in California, I knew this was unusual weather for southern California for that time of year. No one seemed hindered by the rain. Along with the worship and physical downpour, we witnessed many miracles. People were spontaneously, supernaturally being healed and delivered. All over the stadium, people were walking out of their wheelchairs and without their canes. Many deaf had restored hearing and blind were given their sight. People were freed from thoughts of suicide and depression. It was absolutely one of the most beautiful things I had ever witnessed.

Some in the church would argue that God doesn't do miracles today. They would say miracles were for Bible times. There are even some who don't believe the authenticity of Biblical miracles when they read them in the Word. People can argue doctrine and theology all day, but they can't argue with our stories. No one can argue with what we've seen or how we've personally experienced God. However, one of the worst things we can do is limit God to our experiences. He's so much greater than the most amazing thing we've witnessed Him do, and He hasn't changed.

"Jesus Christ is the same yesterday, today, and forever."
Hebrews 13:8

If God is the same for all time, the miracles He did then (when He walked the earth) He's still doing today. We should worship like it, honoring Him for who He is. Jesus: God of the impossible, God of miracles, God who never changes. He neither sleeps nor slumbers. He holds the entire universe in His hands. He loves us intimately. Our worship of Him is for our benefit, not for His. While He is worthy of worship, He doesn't need it. But, we do. Worshiping the living God changes something in us. Jesus is worthy of our devotion, celebration, and thanksgiving.

David delighted in worshiping God, even when his wife criticized his zeal. May we only be concerned about what God thinks of our worship. Regardless of what others might think, we don't look foolish to Him, and that's all that matters. The enemy wants to silence the Bride. Satan would love to stop us from worshipping and speaking up. Some of our most powerful weapons against the schemes of the enemy are to worship God, speak the Word of the Lord and share our testimony.

"My heart was hot within me...While I was musing the fire burned. Then I spoke with my tongue." Psalm 39:3

"Do not be afraid of their faces, For I am with you to deliver you," says the Lord. Then the Lord put forth His hand and touched my mouth, and the Lord said to me: "Behold, I have put My words in your mouth. See, I have this day set you over the nations and over the kingdoms, To root out and to pull down, To destroy and to throw down, To build and to plant. ...Therefore prepare yourself and arise, And speak to them all that I command you. Do not be dismayed before their faces, Lest I dismay you before them." Jeremiah 1:8-10,17

In this hour, God is looking throughout the earth to find messengers who will encourage the world to be reconciled to God and to one another. This is a time of urgency for the truth. We are light-bearers, flame-throwers, ember-blowers, and shooting stars that cannot be snuffed out by the enemy. We were born with a purpose. No matter the assignment, the purpose is the same: we are commissioned as children of the King of kings to be royal priests. The fire of our testimonies can only be kept alive by the oil of the Spirit of God.

"You shall also be a crown of glory in the hand of the Lord, and a royal diadem In the hand of your God." Isaiah 62:3

Prayer:
Lord, fasten us like a peg in your house. Help us to stand for truth, to separate the precious from the vile and be as Your mouth. Make us have foreheads like flint. Cause minds, hearts, and cultures to shift because we've lived on earth. Let it be for Your glory and to prepare the world for Your coming. In Jesus' name. Amen.

CHAPTER THIRTEEN

Take The Land

*"The Lions have their dens up there—The
leopards prowl the glens up there, but
from the top the view is clear of land yet
to be won." (Cant. 4:7,8)
~Hannah Hurnard*

MARY LANCE WAS BILLY Graham's neighbor when they were both growing up in North Carolina. They were the same age, and according to Mary, their families often came together for prayer meetings. Recently in a large gathering in Charlotte, a local pastor shared the story as Mary told it. The families fasted and prayed for a ministry that would bring revival to Charlotte and ultimately take the gospel to the nations. According to Mary, Billy didn't attend their meetings. He thought they were all crazy. Later that same year, he got saved and surrendered his life to Jesus. The rest is history. Mary would frequently share that story, and people would say, "Billy Graham was the fulfillment of that prayer meeting."

Mary would reply, "No. Don't get it wrong. Billy wasn't the fulfillment of that prayer. His life was the seed." In other words, what God used Billy and his team to do during their time on earth planted the seeds for what He is getting ready to do. We haven't seen anything yet.

The pastor shared story after story of heroes in the faith and how their perseverance paved the way for where we are and where we're headed. He captivated a room filled with mighty men and women who have committed their lives and prayers to evangelism, discipleship, and revival.

Interestingly, that morning before going to the meeting, God showed me how Joshua had stood before Israel and had spoken a similar thing. He knew his life was coming to an end. He knew he was leaving a powerful legacy of faithfulness, leadership, and taking the land. He also knew he had been given the privilege to follow in the footsteps of some of the greatest spiritual fathers and military leaders who ever lived. Joshua spoke the word of the Lord and reminded the Israelites from where their fathers had come, and of His faithfulness through it all. As Joshua continued to speak the word of the Lord, he said:

> "I (God) have given you a land for which you did not labor, and cities which you did not build, and you dwell in them; you eat of the vineyards and olive groves which you did not plant.' Joshua 24:13

Joshua spoke this before He exhorted them with his famous words, "Choose for yourselves this day whom you will serve, But as for me and my house, we will serve the Lord" (verse 15). They, too, chose the Lord, and Joshua led all of Israel in renewing their vows to God that day.

My grandpa (my mom's dad) was a Baptist preacher, and I recall sitting at his feet asking questions about God and the Bible. He loved Billy Graham. We would watch the crusades together when they were on television. My life was influenced in a powerful way by the words of God proclaimed through Billy Graham and my Grandpa J.W. They are both heroes of the faith in my life. One had a much more public ministry than the other, but both were valuable to God. What a privilege for me to play in their vineyards and gather a harvest from seeds they've sown.

God chose us to live in such a monumental time on earth, a time of great harvest. There's value in realizing we are reaping benefits from the labor of those who've gone before us. We get to eat from their vineyards and olive trees as well as inherit the land they governed and stewarded. We are not entitled to this. This is a gift. We must honor and steward what previous generations have already planted.

> *"Put in the sickle, for the harvest is ripe. Come, go down; For the winepress is full, The vats overflow—For their wickedness is great.' Multitudes, multitudes in the valley of decision! For the day of the Lord is near in the valley of decision." Joel 3:13-14*

Take the Land of Your Inheritance

Joshua, a mighty man of God, had weighty assignments in taking the land for Israel. As he was stepping into his leadership role, it's no wonder God reminded him not to be afraid.

> *"Have I not commanded you? Be strong and of good courage; do not be afraid, nor be dismayed, for the Lord your God is with you wherever you go." Joshua 1:9*

The LORD told Joshua three times (Joshua 6-9) not to be afraid and He would be with him (Chapters 5 and 9), and God would not leave him or forsake him (Chapter 5). In addition, Moses had already spoken to Joshua about being strong (Deuteronomy 31:6, 7), not to fear (two times in verses 6, 8), the LORD would be with him (verses 6, 8), and God would not leave him nor forsake him (verses 6, 8).

There's a sweet message of rest, confidence and strength here. As we're stepping out into new territory under the leadership of the Holy Spirit, we can trust. There's no need to fear as long as God is leading. We don't need to become anxious about anything. God's got us. If He is for us, who can be against us? The Holy Spirit will lead and make us successful in all we do, if we stay close and follow Him. Fear not!

God exalted Joshua in the sight of Israel to confirm to the people that God was with Joshua just as He was with Moses. God performed many signs and wonders. At God's command, Joshua led Israel across the river Jordan. As the priests, who were bearing the Ark of the Covenant, stepped into the edge of the river, the water receded and all of Israel crossed on dry ground. The children of Israel built a memorial of twelve stones to mark the moment of God's faithfulness.

Following the instructions of the "Commander of the army of the Lord," Joshua told Israel to march around Jericho once each day, without saying a word, while the seven priests were blowing their trumpets. The children of Israel were to do this for six days. On the seventh day they marched around the city seven times in the same way. God often used the number seven to represent completion, perfection, or the fulfillment of something. As they were marching around Jericho the seventh time, at Joshua's command, they shouted when the priests blew their trumpets and the wall of the city fell flat. God gave them victory!

Time after time God used Joshua to lead the Israelite army into battle and to win. They took the land: north, south, east, and west. God made the sun stand still at Joshua's request.

"So the sun stood still, and the moon stopped, till the people had

revenge upon their enemies." Joshua 10:13

In this particular battle, five kings of enemy territories fled in fear to hide in a cave. Joshua killed them and hung them on five trees. The favor of the Lord was with him and Israel had success in battle.

> *"So Joshua took the whole land, according to all that the Lord had said to Moses; and Joshua gave it as an inheritance to Israel according to their divisions by their tribes. Then the land rested from war." Joshua 11:23*

Israel had taken dominion over the land. After a time there were still seven tribes of Israel who hadn't claimed the land of their inheritance. Joshua asked:

> *"How long will you neglect to go and possess the land which the Lord God of your fathers has given you? Pick out from among you three men for each tribe, and I will send them; they shall rise and go through the land, survey it according to their inheritance, and come back to me." Joshua 18:3-4*

God is asking us a similar question. How long will we neglect to go and possess the land He's given us? When will we survey the land to receive our inheritance? Why haven't we stepped into our callings or believed Him for His promises? When will we fully open the gifts we have received from Him? Why haven't we stepped into intimacy with Him? When will we take spiritual dominion through prayer over our own homes, families, workplaces, and communities?

Every place we step, every person we encounter is influenced for God's kingdom. We carry the light of Christ into those places. Ultimately everything belongs to Him anyway. As His children we rightfully own a child's portion. Not many of us would inherit a million dollars and leave it sitting in a bank account, untouched, for our entire lives. We

179

would want to access it, benefit from it, and give a lot of it away. May we learn to receive all that God has for us with open hands and hearts, using it to benefit others and ourselves. As we wisely steward what belongs to us as His children, the world around us will shift.

Into the Hands of a Woman

One particular evening as I stood to speak, I sensed something significant happening in the Spirit. The room was mixed in gender, denomination, race, and generation. Overwhelmed by the weight of it all, I imagined myself outfitted in stealthy armor and lots of leather, hair flowing in the wind (of course), swords in my belt, riding on a fierce horse into an unknown territory that was part of my birthright. I was taking the land of my inheritance.

Most of my life had been spent believing God couldn't and wouldn't use me to speak His truth, especially not if men were in hearing distance. From the time I was young I had always said to myself, "If I had been a boy I would've been a preacher." It's funny, because for years on both sides of my family I was the only female—all my cousins are males. On my mom's side many of my cousins have become pastors. It's part of our family inheritance since my grandpa was also a pastor.

Once while visiting alone at Mary, my friend's, cabin in northern California, the Lord spoke sweet things to me about my calling. During this special time He said, "Rivera many are called but few are chosen. I'm not going to use you in spite of you being a woman; I'm going to use you because you are a woman. You've been born at this time in history for a special purpose."

If God speaks something like this to us in private, He doesn't just stop there. If He knows we are struggling with really believing Him, He'll bring people along to confirm what He's said. In this situation He had to bring in some heavy reinforcements. Men! But, not just any men. God chose to use men who didn't know me at all, and who had never even seen me. Only God could orchestrate such a thing! While I was at the cabin, I became ill. I knew there was a body of believers down the mountain who believed in God's ability to heal. They also flowed in the prophetic gift. That means most of them were accustomed to hearing the voice of God, and speaking it out. God convinced me to go to this church for prayer. I thought, "Why not?" As I was driving down the mountain my sinuses cleared. I asked, "Lord, why would You ask me to come all the way down the mountain to this church, if You knew You were going to heal me before I got there?" The first step out the door was a demonstration of faith. Sometimes He wants us to step into our healing.

Curiosity about the way they do ministry led me on. I visited their healing room where I witnessed faith, prayer, and a lot of solid Bible teaching on the subject. Besides that, I saw several people testify to being healed. At this point, we were all in a class together to follow up after the healing room time. My uncertainties vanished as I witnessed an old woman, probably in her eighties, with scoliosis and one leg shorter than the other being healed. People in my group prayed for her and God literally grew her shorter leg longer. Her curved back began straightening. Her entire adult life had been spent with a twisted body and God was healing it. With a huge smile and tears, she hugged her family and the ones who had prayed. The way she walked was straighter and she stood tall with hope. My eyes had never seen anything quite like it. Sadly, if I hadn't seen it I'm not sure I would have believied it.

Throughout my time there, several men spoke words that affirmed my calling. One by one they confirmed God's promises over my life. Some of these men were even visiting from out of town, and God used them all to say what He knew I needed to hear. They spoke His words, not their own.

The first one was a teacher in the healing room. He said, "This is a new one. I've never heard this before. I'm hearing the Lord say 'feet.' The shoes of the gospel of peace. Beautiful are the feet that carry the good news. Someone in this room is called to preach the gospel." As though I was not in control of my own body and responses, I started crying uncontrollably. God's presence was so heavy. I couldn't stop the tears. Those who know me know I'm not one to cry a lot. I hesitantly raised my hand as if it wasn't already obvious to the teacher. He prayed for me, to bless and declare that calling over me.

The second person spoke to me after worship the next day. When I walked in to attend their weekend service, the seats appeared to be full. I thought I had missed my opportunity to sit in the service but the Holy Spirit said, "Go to the front." So I did. When I turned to my right, I recognized three people I had seen the previous day in the healing rooms. One of them, Cyrus, had prayed for the elderly lady. He smiled and motioned that there was one seat open behind them. After worship, two men in the group asked if they could pray for me and I agreed to it. As they prayed Cyrus spoke specifics regarding the promises of God over my life.

Immediately following Cyrus' prayer (between worship and the message), the pastor stood to talk. This pastor is known all over the world, and he said, "We're going to start things a little differently this morning. When I woke up today, God said there would be some people with us who have never been here before and may not be back. He told me to commission them to do what He's called them to do. If that is you, would you please stand up?"

My heart was beating fast enough to race out of my chest. I couldn't believe what I was hearing. I knew it was me. God was using a man in ministry, who had no idea what God had said about me, to commission me into my calling. God didn't need this pastor to make it official, but apparently He thought I did. Admittedly it did confirm it even more. God tore down strongholds that weekend. He used seemingly random men to speak my calling over me. Apparently if God can use a donkey, He can use a woman to be His instrument to speak to the people. He changed my mind about who I am. He used men to solidify my purpose in my own heart and mind. Only He could do that!

> *"There is neither Jew nor Greek, there is neither slave nor free, there is neither male nor female; for you are all one in Christ Jesus." Galatians 3:28*

Many still have the mindset that women's roles in the church should consist of teaching the children and cooking for potlucks. Many would say a woman shouldn't preach, teach, or lead other adults, especially if men are present. What a waste of God's spiritual gifts to so many women in the church. And really, how sad for the great number of men who are missing out on what God has to offer them through gifted women. Jesus told the disciples:

> *"All authority has been given to Me in heaven and on earth. Go therefore and make disciples of all the nations, baptizing them in the name of the Father and of the Son and of the Holy Spirit, teaching them to observe all things that I have commanded you; and lo, I am with you always, even to the end of the age.' Amen." Matthew 28:18-20*

Assuming this Word is true (since all of God's Word is truth), we as women are not going to stand before God and be questioned for speaking on His behalf. He's not going to ask us, "Why did you tell them who I Am? Why did you tell them how much I love them? Why did you share about My faithfulness to you?"

We've all been given necessary and useful gifts from God. We have to learn to work together as one body part does with another. A woman who has been given the gifts of teaching and leadership should be able to help the body with her strengths. We don't choose our gifts. The nature of a gift is that it comes without our choosing or deserving. Jesus told them to go into the nations to make disciples, baptizing them.

Then He said, *"Teach them (people) to observe all things that I have commanded you."* Whatever He taught the disciples to do He also wants us to do. These weren't optional. They were things He had commanded.

> *"Very truly I tell you, whoever believes in me will do the works I have been doing, and they will do even greater things than these, because I am going to the Father. And I will do whatever you ask in my name, so that the Father may be glorified in the Son. You may ask me for anything in my name, and I will do it."*
> *John 14:12-14 (NIV)*

We are not greater than Jesus, but He indicated here that as His disciples (or students), we would do GREATER things than these. If we're ambassadors of Christ, (re)presenting Him, we'll do what He did regardless of our gender. He didn't tell "men only" to do these things. He was speaking to all of us. He said, *"Go therefore...."* He didn't say, "'Men, go therefore'... or 'Women, go therefore....'" He just said, *"Go."*

Like the parable of the servants and talents, I want to stand before God and hear Him say, "Well done." Don't you? I certainly don't want to hear Him ask, "Why didn't you...?" Living to please God, not for the acceptance and praise of men, is the only sure way to live. Why would we want to live any other way? What we do of eternal value is the only thing that will last. Everything else is temporal and fleeting.

Barak, the commander of the Israelite army, knew a good thing when he saw it. He wasn't afraid to team up and work with a woman, especially one like Deborah. She was exemplary of a strong, yet God-fearing woman. God used her to shift culture and the trajectory of an entire country.

If we read Deborah's story in Judges 4, we discover several things about her life. She was a prophetess, meaning she heard the voice of God clearly and did what He said. She was wife to Lapidoth, so she had marital and household responsibilities. Last but not least, she was a judge in Israel. She lived in a time before Israel appointed earthly kings to lead them. Her role as judge was equivalent to being the president of the United States. God actually chose a woman to govern His people. That puts what God thinks of women in leadership roles into perspective, doesn't it?

Jabin, king of Canaan, had oppressed Israel for twenty years. This would be equivalent to the United States being handed over to twenty years of harsh treatment by our worst enemy. From reading her story, we can conclude that Deborah had enough. Her irritation became part of her story. God told her to send Israel into battle to defeat this wicked enemy. She told Barak what the Lord had spoken to her, because that's what prophetesses do.

> *"The Lord, the God of Israel, commands you: 'Go, take with you ten thousand men of Naphtali and Zebulun and lead them up to Mount Tabor. I will lead Sisera, the commander of Jabin's army, with his chariots and his troops to the Kishon River and give him into your hands.'" Judges 4:6-7 (NIV)*

Barak said he would go, but only if she went with him. Barak knew

Deborah heard God's voice clearly. Perhaps he thought that if she was willing to risk her own life in the battle with him, then she must have been certain of what she heard from God.

> *"So she said, 'I will surely go with you; nevertheless there will be no glory for you in the journey you are taking, for the Lord will sell Sisera into the hand of a woman.'" (verse 9a)*

The morning came for battle and Deborah encouraged Barak with another prophetic declaration, "Up! For this is the day in which the Lord has delivered Sisera into your hand. Has not the Lord gone out before you? (verse 14)." Deborah was a great leader because of the One she was following. The greatest leaders follow the Leader of all leaders.

Barak pursued the enemy and all of Sisera's army fell by the sword. Not a man was left. However, Sisera slipped away from the battle on foot. He found Jael's tent and thought she might cover for him. Oh, she covered for him all right! She covered him with a blanket and gave him milk to drink. Then she used a hammer to drive a tent peg through his temple. Deborah was right! God did give the enemy over to a woman, and her name was Jael.

Willing to Wage War

Almost nothing is more irritating than flies, gnats, or bees buzzing near my face. Flies are nasty, disease-carrying, feces-eating little creatures. Bees really hurt if they sting, and they can be dangerous. Gnats are just annoying. If any of these get into my house, I warn them and try to fan them towards an open door. If they don't soon find their way out, they die.

Deborah was not afraid to fight. The enemy had pushed her to her limits. They had been in her country's personal space far too long. She knew God was ready to set His people free. She had spent enough time in secret with Him to know He was trustworthy. She knew she carried the authority from God to call forth Israel's victory and win. Jael's situation was a little different. The enemy came into her house. She did what I do with those flying insects. She smashed his head.

There's never victory without a battle. Anytime God asks us to do something big there is going to be a battle. Technically, Jesus already won our battles on the cross. We've already won before the fight begins. Don't be afraid to fight, especially on your knees. Be willing to step out and willing to pray with fierce persistence. Satan wants to destroy us. But Jesus said:

> "I have given you authority to trample on snakes and scorpions and to overcome all the power of the enemy; nothing will harm you." Luke 10:19 (NIV)

We have the spiritual authority to overcome ALL the power of the enemy. Nothing will harm us. No. Thing. We get to govern our own houses, families, and God-given territories. We've inherited land from the Lord whether we realize it or not. Will we fight for what matters most? The value of the spoils often determines how hard we fight. Who's fighting harder for your people, your purity, your marriage, your destiny, and your calling—you or the enemy? The enemy will come into our literal homes to try to divide, destroy, deceive, and build strongholds. A stronghold is a wall built around a lie.

Isaiah 54: 17 says: "'No weapon formed against you shall prosper, And every tongue which rises against you in judgment You shall condemn. This is the heritage of the servants of the Lord, And their

187

righteousness is from Me,' Says the Lord."

As children of God, it is our *heritage* (inheritance) to condemn any tongue that rises against us. So when the enemy comes at us with a lie, we not only get to say no to it, we get to condemn it. When he whispers we're not good enough, when another person speaks a word against us, or when sickness and depression try to creep in, we get to say no. Curse the curse.

The enemy has no power over us until we come into an agreement with him. In the garden, God had been clear about His will and His boundaries. Eve's fall occurred and sin entered when she entertained Satan. She listened to his lies, she talked to him, she believed him, then she acted on what she believed. For example, fear has no power in our lives until we make an agreement with it. When we choose to say no to fear and yes to confidence in God, we dismantle the enemy's plans to try to immobilize and silence us. *If God is for us, who can be against us? (Romans 8:31b).* We can take authority in prayer to tear down strongholds: pornography, lust, greed, depression, fear, division, addiction, sickness and so on.

> *"For though we live in the world, we do not wage war as the world does. The weapons we fight with are not the weapons of the world. On the contrary, they have divine power to demolish strongholds. We demolish arguments and every pretension that sets itself up against the knowledge of God, and we take captive every thought to make it obedient to Christ." 2 Corinthians 10:3-5 (NIV)*

Don't be disillusioned by the tactics of the enemy. Opposition is not an excuse to quit but permission to fight. It's confirmation that we're on the right track.

Positioned to Win

Deborah was a leader of leaders. She realized and utilized her position. She had great influence and favor with leaders and people in general. She was positioned to lead men into a history changing battle. Deborah understood teamwork. It wasn't all about her. It was about winning for God and country. It was about His glory being revealed and His victory for Israel. Confident in her own skin, Deborah was willing to set other people up for the win and celebrate when they succeeded.

Jael was hidden in the privacy of her tent and God allowed her assignment to come to her. She didn't have to strive, or go looking to try to fulfill her destiny. It came to her. Our callings are often in the privacy of our home, staring us in the face. Our greatest assignments are sometimes the ones found in the middle of mundane, ordinary routines. Don't give up if you're in a hidden season raising children, or whatever the situation may be. God can still fulfill your destiny, right there.

Barak was a man of valor, extremely intelligent, and willing to work alongside a woman for Israel's victory. And what a win it was! He and Deborah sang together in celebration after their triumph.

> *"Deborah and Barak the son of Abinoam sang on that day, saying: 'When leaders lead in Israel, When the people willingly offer themselves, Bless the Lord!'" Judges 5:1-2*

Yes. What a beautiful scene when men and women in the Body come together as leaders and work for the win! How pleasing to God that is. The fact remains, when we stand before Him, we are going to be held accountable for how and why we've done what we've done on earth. Hopefully when He searches us He will find our motives have been pure and our actions have been propelled by our desire to please Him and not by selfish ambition.

In Isaiah 22, the Lord removed Shebna from his powerful position because he had misused it for evil. God replaced him with his humble servant Eliakim. Verse 22 speaks of Eliakim saying:

> "*The key of the house of David I will lay on his shoulder; So he shall open, and no one shall shut; And he shall shut, and no one shall open.*"

This scripture is also a type, or copy, and shadow representing (or symbolic of) Jesus:

> "*I will fasten him as a peg in a secure place, and he will become a glorious throne to his father's house. 'They will hang on him all the glory of his father's house.*" Isaiah 22:23

Eliakim was positioned and given the key to govern the house of David. God is taking down the Shebnas and lifting up the Eliakims. In this hour, God is looking throughout the earth for ones He can trust. He is raising up an army of Eliakims to take their place of authority. We are being given the keys from God to open and close gates and doors in the spirit: *to open so that no one can shut, and shut so that no one can open.*

Each of us has been appointed to different territories or spheres of influence. For example, some are in governmental offices while others are working on college campuses to see God's glory revealed. God has given us land as our inheritance. May we govern it with Holy Spirit boldness and authority.

Ask Him to give spiritual eyes to see how to open and close the gates of our own homes, cities and territories. As leaders, ask for wisdom in what to bring in and what to move out, who to raise up, and who to dismantle. May our only agenda be to carry out His.

Many are taking new land. In a new season we find ourselves in uncharted territory. We are feeling excited yet unsettled. God has helped us win battles to get here. Now it's time to steward the land. Ask God how He wants you to care for what He's given. May He continually increase our territories for His glory.

In the words of Paul, *"Take heed to the ministry which you have received in the Lord, that you may fulfill it."* Colossians 4:17

God is establishing a generation who will not take no for an answer. These are the men and women who are after the heart of God, ones willing to go before Him to prepare the way for His coming. Men and women who love, worship, listen to, and obey God. They are courageous to say yes, and willing to step up and out of their comfort zones. Like Jael, they may not have much, but God has a plan to utilize what little they have to offer. Being who God created them to be, they each have unique value and purpose. Like Deborah, they are willing to fight in the trenches and are open to setting others up for success. Humble, yet God-confident, they are men and women who will help ready the Bride and bring this next great awakening. Willing to let go of the past to take hold of their future, they are taking the land of their inheritance.

> *"Ask of Me, and I will give You the nations for Your inheritance,*
> *And the ends of the earth for Your possession."* Psalm 2:8

Prayer:
Father, Thank you for giving us spiritual authority over all the power of the enemy. Thank you for the gift of our inheritance. Thank you for trusting us with vineyards and land we didn't plant. We have the privilege of reaping a harvest where we haven't sown. Give us

courage, boldness and wisdom to steward well what you've given us. Help us to continue to take back the land that rightfully belongs to you and your children! In Jesus' name. Amen.

CHAPTER FOURTEEN

Now Is The Time

"Never leave till tomorrow that which you can do today."
~ Benjamin Franklin

WE ALL HAVE HAD occasions that we would have loved to capture forever, moments when we wished time stood still. The beauty of a garland made of fresh cut evergreen boughs or a table set to perfection with colorful, carefully strewn flowers. Snow as it falls and quietly covers the ground. The smell of roasting marshmallows around a crackling campfire. A baby freshly birthed and bathed. Sunsets and sunrises peeking through the clouds. Music that moves us to dance, or tears. The exhilaration of long walks. Picking wildflowers. Overcoming fears. Loving and being loved. The sky painted with bursts of pink and yellow light. The wind and leaves rustling in fall. The smell of the ocean. Hearing children giggle, especially our own. Old men and women who still hold hands. The delight of friendship. The overwhelming comfort of long-awaited, warm hugs. These timeless treasures of life on earth are all around us for the savoring, and just a taste of what heaven will be like.

My dear friend would jokingly say, "If I'd known I was going to live so long I would've taken better care of myself." She has since passed on and I'm so much richer for having known her. Life is brief. One thing will always remain certain—change. Things change, and life goes on. Moments can't be contained except in pictures, words, or the far corners of our minds. Don't let them pass by. Engage in the moments. Be present. Lay down the devices and vices. Look people square in the eyes and smile at them. Love and listen intently. One day you may not have them or they may not have you. If the sum of our minutes make up our days, and the sum of our days make up our lives, will we have spent ourselves on anything of value? Will its value be lasting or eternal? Every new season is an opportunity to adventure with God! Now is the time to make each day count.

For Such A Time As This

Esther made each day count. We know from Esther Chapter 1, she went through a time of preparation in the palace. The king favored Esther and she was chosen to be queen. She knew she was positioned for a specific role at a crucial time in history.

> "For if you remain completely silent at this time, relief and deliverance will arise for the Jews from another place, but you and your father's house will perish. Yet who knows whether you have come to the kingdom for such a time as this?" Esther 4:14

Mordecai was Esther's cousin who sent word to her that the king had signed a decree to annihilate the Jews. The king's right-hand man, Haman, hated the Jews and had devised this plan. Mordecai's message told Queen Esther to go to the king and plead before him for her people, the Jews. Esther knew that anyone, including herself, who went to the king without being invited was risking his or her life. But, remaining silent was also risking her life. Either way, Esther would put her life on the line. Esther had to face her fears. This queen thing wasn't all it was cracked up to be. Esther said yes to the assignment. She knew if she died, at least she would die trying.

God has positioned you and me, like Esther, strategically in this particular time and place in history. We may even feel that our situation is less than ideal. Be assured, we have purpose beyond what we can see. God has been speaking ot me, saying, "Your willingness to do what you can't do is the very thing that qualifies you to do it!! I'm the One who qualifies. You can't, but I can." This word is for you too. Merely saying yes isn't enough. It will take courage, sacrifice, and total surrender. But as we follow God step by step, He qualifies and equips us with all that we need.

Obedience to God doesn't always look polished. The world, more than likely, won't understand it. Willingness to follow God may not look the way we think it should. It may not always be fireworks and a big show. Sometimes what God asks of us is quite simple. We can rest in the fact that He knows best.

Esther certainly wouldn't have chosen the predicament in which she found herself. She laid down all expectation except of what God could and would do. She yielded to the providential plan of God. Esther called her people to three days of fasting and prayer. She didn't expect those under her influence and leadership to do something she wasn't willing to do herself. She fasted and prayed for three days with them. Esther had the reverential fear of the Lord. She knew if anyone could get her out of this mess, it was Him.

"Charm is deceitful and beauty is passing, But a woman who fears the Lord, she shall be praised." Proverbs 31:30

We, especially as women, struggle with expectation. We have expectations of God and people and don't communicate them half the time. Then when our desires aren't met we find ourselves irritated, vulnerable, and disappointed. The only One worthy of our expectation is Jesus. Esther went in to see the king without an official invitation. He loved Esther, so she was given favor with him.

> "So it was, when the king saw Queen Esther standing in the court, that she found favor in his sight, and the king held out to Esther the golden scepter that was in his hand. Then Esther went near and touched the top of the scepter. And the king said to her, 'What do you wish, Queen Esther? What is your request? It shall be given to you—up to half the kingdom!'" Esther 5:2-3

He told her up to half the kingdom was hers; all she had to do was ask. She invited the king and Haman to a banquet. They accepted her invitation. At the banquet, the king told her the same thing again. He asked her to tell him her request and stated again that up to half the kingdom was hers. She stalled and invited them to another banquet the next day.

Timing is everything. If you're married, remember that some requests and conversations need the proper timing. Esther was wise. She used discernment from God to determine the right time for presenting her request. Esther wasn't manipulating him, but I'm sure the suspense was useful in keeping the king's attention. Men enjoy suspense and mystery. Speaking of mystery, if you aren't married yet, leave something for his imagination. Cover up and save yourself for your marriage. Don't let everyone see what God meant for your husband only. There's something mysterious and intriguing in giving your future husband something to look forward to.

On the day of Esther's second banquet with the king and Haman, as the king and Haman were dining with Queen Esther, the king again asked Queen Esther to tell him her request. This meant for a total of three times, the king said essentially the same thing, *"What is your petition, Queen Esther? It shall be granted you. And what is your request, up to half the kingdom? It shall be done!"*

> *"Then Queen Esther answered and said, 'If I have found favor in your sight, O king, and if it pleases the king, let my life be given me at my petition, and my people at my request. For we have been sold, my people and I, to be destroyed, to be killed, and to be annihilated. Had we been sold as male and female slaves, I would have held my tongue, although the enemy could never compensate for the king's loss.'*
>
> *So King Ahasuerus answered and said to Queen Esther, 'Who is he, and where is he, who would dare presume in his heart to do such a thing?'*
>
> *And Esther said, 'The adversary and enemy is this wicked Haman!'"*
> Esther 7:3-6

She was seated at a table in the presence of her enemy. With great courage, she called Haman out and won the battle. The king was enraged and had Haman hung on his own gallows, the ones he had built to hang Mordecai. Haman's decree regarding the Jews, according to law, should not have been able to be revoked. The king gave Queen Esther and Mordecai authority to write a new law giving the Jews the right to gather together, protect, and avenge themselves from their enemies. Then the king told them to seal it with his signet ring, which was a seal of authority.

> *"You yourselves write a decree concerning the Jews, as you please, in the king's name, and seal it with the king's signet ring; for whatever is written in the king's name and sealed with the*

king's signet ring no one can revoke." Esther 8:8

Mordecai wrote a new law, allowing the Jews in every city to gather together and avenge themselves on their enemies. On the very day the enemies of the Jews had hoped to overpower them, the opposite occurred. The Jews overpowered those who hated them. Mordecai, with the king's authority, decreed a new thing over the people of God and it came to pass.

Similarly, we belong to the King of all kings. We have been sealed with the promise of the Holy Spirit (Ephesians 1). He has extended His royal scepter to us and is saying, "Make your request known. The Kingdom is yours!" We are loved and favored by Him as Esther was in this story. We've been given a table with our King in the presence of our enemies. We can rise up with confidence that God will hang the enemy on his own gallows. When we choose to dine with our King and feast from His table, this is truly how we win our biggest battles. Intimacy with God is a major key to governing and winning. In that place He downloads us with strategy from heaven. We've been granted the authority through the Holy Spirit to write laws, to govern, to decree a thing, and then to see it come to pass. Like Esther and Mordecai, we will make our enemy tremble. We will be men and women who cause Satan to shudder when he sees our feet hit the ground.

Times and Seasons

A special friend of mine was praying with me when she saw a picture of a woman holding a huge sword. She said, "I see her standing tall with a big sword in both hands. Muscles are bulging. Her feet are planted at shoulder width in a strong stance. She's been holding this sword a long time. It's ready. She'll use it at God's command. Her gaze is intense, steady and fixed on Him. That's the strength for holding it. The sword is big and pointing straight up. She's learned how to hold it. She's waiting for instructions from the Lord to use it." The next day after her vision, I opened my Bible and my eyes fell on this.

> *"Swords at the ready! Thrust right! Set your blade! Thrust left—Wherever your edge is ordered!" Ezekiel 21:16*

It was as if those words jumped off the page to have me read them. This was a powerful example of the Word of God being alive, active, and sharper than a double-edged sword. There it was. There He was. The Word was alive and confirming what my friend had seen in the vision.

The sword of the Spirit is God's Word. The sword is also a weapon used in battle to dismantle the power of the enemy. Her vision was a picture of being equipped with readiness for battle, by the power of God's Spirit and His Word. The woman's perseverance to hold this huge weapon was from God. He was showing the power of waiting to hear Him before moving the sword. Before speaking a word or moving forward in battle, she waited for His orders.

On the Jewish calendar, 2017 is the year 5777. It's important to know the time in which we're living and ask God to help us navigate the times wisely, as Issachar did in the Old Testament.

> *"The sons of Issachar who had understanding of the times, to know what Israel ought to do, their chiefs were two hundred; and all their brethren were at their command." 1 Chronicles 12:32*

In Hebrew, a number is also a letter and vice versa. So, 5777 is divided and interpreted as:

5700 = "The year of"

70 = "Ayin" = eye

7 = "Zayin" = Sword (pictograph) = Vav (tent peg) with a crown on top (classical Hebrew script). It is also the number of completion or perfection.

Crown

Vav

Can you believe we are now in the year of the sword, literally? This is "the year of...the eye...and the sword (the vav with a crown on top.)"

"Ayin," is the season of the eye. God wants to increase our ability to see in ways we never have before. Seventy was significant in Numbers 11. God poured out his Spirit on the 70 elders in Israel and they prophesied. Also, in Luke 10, Jesus sent 70 to heal the sick, cast out demons, and proclaim the kingdom. It's a time when God wants to release us by His Spirit to see signs and wonders.

A vav is a connecting pin that holds things together. It looks like the nails used on train tracks. They were the connecting pins used in the tent of meeting in the Old Testament to hold the tent together. It's also a peg. It's the tent peg that Jael used to drive through the temple of Sisera, the enemy, in the story of Deborah. It's a holding pen, a stake, and a weapon. The crown on the top signifies royalty. It's a year of war, connecting, and royalty. It's a season of greater revelation of the kingdom and increased authority. We've been seated in a position of royalty and have been given all that we need to take authority in the battles we face.

The sword represents battle and the Word. The sword of the Spirit is the Word of God. It's one of our greatest weapons against the enemy. This year battles will be won! The church is divided. There are two camps: those who major on the Spirit and His gifts, and those who major on the Word and tradition. This will be a year of unity where the Body of Christ will begin to come together. The two camps that focus on Spirit and Word will converge to see God lifted up. We will see Him in power. When God's people lay down differences and come together as one, He releases blessing and pours out His Spirit.

> *"The key of the house of David I will lay on his shoulder; So he shall open, and no one shall shut; And he shall shut, and no one shall open. I will fasten him as a peg in a secure place, And he will become a glorious throne to his father's house. ...In that day,' says the Lord of hosts, 'the peg that is fastened in the secure place will be removed and be cut down and fall, and the burden that was on it will be cut off; for the Lord has spoken.'" Isaiah 22: 22–25*

This year of seven, Zayin, and its classical Hebrew script of a vav with a crown on it is Jesus. He was vav(ed), or nailed, to the cross for our sins with a crown on His head. It's the year of Jesus! There will be greater revelation of Jesus. Holy Spirit reveals Jesus. And Jesus reveals the Father. More than ever Jesus will be manifest on the earth through His people, and eyes long shut will be opened to see.

Today

> *"But encourage one another daily, as long as it is called 'Today,' so that none of you may be hardened by sin's deceitfulness." Hebrews 3:13 (NIV)*

Remember Paul and Silas? They seized the day with praises in the midst of imprisonment. The prisoners were listening. After the earthquake shook the foundations, and loosed the prisoners, the prison guard woke up and saw that the prison doors were open. He thought the prisoners had escaped and he was ready to take his own life when Paul stopped him. Grateful, he knelt in front of them and asked what he must do to be saved.

> *"So they said, 'Believe on the Lord Jesus Christ, and you will be saved, you and your household.' Then they spoke the word of the Lord to him and to all who were in his house." Acts 16:31-32*

He took them into his home, washed their stripes (lacerations), fed them, and rejoiced with them. He and his entire household believed on Jesus. This is what happens when we rejoice under trial and choose to praise Him in prison. When we open our mouths to sing and speak the truth within hearing distance of those who may have never heard it, chains are broken, and doors are opened.

If we're willing to make time for the one, entire households can be shifted. God is as interested in us taking time for one over coffee and scones as He is in us reaching thousands on a stadium platform. One by one, being won by One, is how we change the world. That's not to say God may not give us opportunities to speak to large crowds. If He does, certainly we should seize those opportunities, as Peter did. After the Holy Spirit had come on him in power at Pentecost, he spoke and 3,000 souls were added to the kingdom in a moment. Peter told them about Jesus and the resurrection. They also asked what to do to be saved. Then Peter said to them:

> *"Repent, and let every one of you be baptized in the name of Jesus Christ for the remission of sins; and you shall receive the gift of the Holy Spirit. For the promise is to you and to your children, and to all who are afar off, as many as the Lord our God will call." Acts 2:38-39*

Those who believed were baptized. They all broke bread together and had many things in common. They were one in Spirit, and the Lord *"added to the church daily those who were being saved"* *(verse 47).* There's no time like the present to take time for people. There's no gift like our presence, infused with His, to give away.

NOW IS THE TIME.

Prayer of Faith

Perhaps you are reading this and you can't recall a time of personally believing on Jesus to be your Lord and Savior. I would love to lead you in a prayer to do just that. Of course the prayer doesn't change you, only your faith and relationship with Jesus does. A really great place to start is communicating to God the desire of your heart to be a part of His family and be in relationship with Him. A simple prayer gives you a place to go back to if the enemy ever tries to tell you it never happened, or that you don't belong.

Jesus, I confess my sin to you. I ask you to forgive me. Free me from it. Heal me from my past. I believe you died on the cross and were raised to life so my sins could be erased. You died so I could have eternal life and have a relationship with my heavenly Father, I ask You to breathe new life in me by Your Spirit. I invite You to save me, lead my life, and bring me into a personal relationship with You now and always. Thank You for loving me and forgiving me of my sins. Show me how to live my life for You. Amen.

"Now is the accepted time; behold, now is the day of salvation."
2 Corinthians 6:2b

With a simple but genuine prayer your slate is wiped clean. God just hit delete on the hidden history of your life, to never remember it or bring it up again. He loves you dearly. Today is the beginning of the rest and best days of your everlasting life.

"Those who are wise shall shine Like the brightness of the firmament, And those who *turn many to righteousness, Like the stars forever and ever."* Daniel 12:3

Epilogue

To be clear, I've never written anything in my life with more conviction. I saw God with each page of this process. He revealed Himself and confirmed every part. There were times that I literally would finish writing and take a deep, cleansing breath with a keen awareness that I did not scribe these words on my own. I was merely working alongside a generous, creative Helper.

I realize that some of what I've written is going to stretch some people out of their comfort zones. It would never be my intention to write anything that would cause confusion or division. Rather, I believe God wanted this book written to shed the light of revelation on some long misunderstood principles in His Word. This book was written to be a bridge to hopefully bring the divided camps in the church together. It was written to shift perspectives about God and our role as His children.

God is God. He is very clear that He cannot be contained. He has not changed, nor will He ever. It's time we take Him out of the tidy little box we've put Him in for far too long. And honestly, why would we want to confine Him? He's God and so much more capable and well equipped than we are.

Blessed be the name of the Lord. Let us lay aside our differences and praise His holy name together!

Rivera

Thank you,

David, you love, encourage and sacrifice more than any human I have ever known. I love you. Words definitely are not enough.

Hunter and Haley, God knew just what I needed when He gave me you--priceless treasures. Your laughter, encouragement, and patience spur me on.

Mom and Dad, you've supported and believed in me, always. I love you both.

Keith, Jo (and Finley), you inspire me as you continually and lovingly demonstrate the value of family.

Dan, the word you gave me was spot on. Thank you for your sensitivity to the Spirit and obedience to give it.

Carole Ann and Laurie, what would I do without you? (I never want to find out!) You have believed in God's dreams for me before I believed them myself. You have held me up with friendship, prayer and encouragement at times when I didn't think I could continue on in this process. I love you both.

Carol McCall, Audrey Malloy, Joanna Adkins, Elizabeth Loebs, Tavitris Bracey, Donna and Evan Loebs, Laurie and Jeff Glascock, Lara and Jess Hill, Susan and Dayne Pierantoni, Mikha'el Pham, Geri Gardner, Rita Barbeau, Helen Goldman, and Katie Hauser your prayers, encouragement, friendship and partnership helped make this possible.

All of you who so graciously allowed me to use your stories, I pray God uses them to change lives.

Kayce Ogburn, your generosity is astounding. I will never forget my weeks writing at your Beach Haven.

Carol McCall, Carole Ann Loebs, Denise Sicking, Dana Ward, and Lara Hill, you all have an impeccable eye for detail. Thank you.

Mary, Fonda, Carol, Rebecca, Cindy, and Brenda: As we sat on a blanket and I read aloud from my first book (per your request), God stirred something in me again for writing. We never know how we might inspire one another, do we?

Joshua Hildebrand, you are such a kind, humble soul. What a fun couple of days filming. Thanks for your patience and going the extra mile with me to make the video a success.

Markus Alison, the book cover is just perfect.

Joel Stenkvist, the photo is amazing. Your trip to the Preacher's Pulpit was timely.

Every person who reached out to tell me you were praying for me through this process, you blessed me immensely! I could not have done this without your prayers. (You know who you are.)

Notes

Angelou, Maya. *Goodreads.Com*, 2017, http://www.goodreads.com/author/quotes/3503.Maya_Angelo u.

Aylward, Gladys. "Gladys Aylward Quote". *A-Z Quotes*, 2017, http://www.azquotes.com/quote/697844.

Bonnke, Reinhard. *Even Greater*. Orlando, Fla., Full Flame, 2004,.

Boom, Corrie ten. "A Quote By Corrie Ten Boom". *Goodreads*, 2017, http://www.goodreads.com/quotes/254564-there-is-no-pit-so-deep-that-god-s-love-is.

Chapman, Steven C. "Dive". Sparrow Records, Brentwood, TN, 1999.

Gove, Philip Babcock. *Webster's Third New International Dictionary Of The English Language, Unabridged*. 1st ed., Springfield, Mass., Merriam-Webster, 1993.

Hurnard, Hannah and Darien B Cooper. *Hinds' Feet On High Places*. Shippensburg, PA, Destiny Image Publishers, 2005,.

Jamison, Christopher. *Monastic Steps For A Fulfilling Life*. 1st ed., London, Weidenfeld & Nicolson, 2008,.

"Jeanne D'arc Quotes (Author Of Joan Of Arc) 1411-1431". *Goodreads.Com*, 2017, http://www.goodreads.com/author/quotes/1509101.Jeanne_d _Arc.

"Kingdom". *Merriam-Webster.Com*, 2017,

https://www.merriam-webster.com/dictionary/kingdom.

LeClaire, Jennifer. "4 Things To Do If You Can'T Hear God'S Voice". *Charisma News*, 2017, http://www.charismanews.com/opinion/47829-4-things-to-do-if-you-can-t-hear-god-s-voice.

"Loose". *Merriam-Webster.Com*, 2017, https://www.merriam-webster.com/dictionary/loose.

"Luke 3:16 KJV". *Blue Letter Bible*, 2017, https://www.blueletterbible.org/lang/lexicon/lexicon.cfm?Strongs=G907&t=KJV.

Nitzsche, Jack et al. "Up Where We Belong". Island, 1982, https://en.wikipedia.org/wiki/Up_Where_We_Belong.

Parsons, John J. "The Letter Zayin". *Hebrew4christians.Com*, 2017, http://www.hebrew4christians.com/Grammar/Unit_One/Aleph-Bet/Zayin/zayin.html.

Pitre, Isaac. "Show ISAAC PITRE Divine DNA1". *YouTube*. N.p., 2013. Web. 17 Sept. 2016.

Roberts, Frances J. *Come Away My Beloved*. 1st ed., Uhrichsville, Ohio, Barbour Pub., 2002,.

Robinson, Robert. "Come Thou Fount Of Every Blessing (1757)". *En.Wikipedia.Org*, 2017, https://en.wikipedia.org/wiki/Come_Thou_Fount_of_Every_Blessing.

LeStrange, Ryan. *Divine Connections, Disconnections, And Reconnections*. 2016. Web. 1 Feb. 2016.

Schaeffer, Francis A. "Francis A. Schaeffer Quotes (Author Of How Should We Then Live? The Rise And Decline Of Western Thought And Culture) (Page 2 Of 4)". *Goodreads.Com*, 2017, http://www.goodreads.com/author/quotes/7491463.Francis_A _Schaeffer?page=2

Ugolino, and William Heywood. *The Little Flowers Of St Francis Of Assisi*. 1st ed., New York, Vintage, 1998,.

Wesley, John. "A Quote By John Wesley". *Goodreads*, 2017, http://www.goodreads.com/quotes/137786-give-me-one-hundred-preachers-who-fear-nothing-but-sin.

About The Author

On most mornings you can find Rivera Douthit at her country home in North Carolina sipping coffee on her front porch rocker. She is wife to one amazing man and mama to two beautifully creative children. Since she couldn't keep the goldfish alive, she has no pets. From a wife-beater tank in the morning to heels in the evening, Rivera is poised in various situations with all types of people. She loves relationships (new and old), the arts, nature, and has a genuine way of seeing God in all of it.

Rivera is founder of Gonia Global, a ministry designed to bring evangelism and revival to the nations. Her past experience as a Critical Care nurse has shaped her as a clear and effective communicator with a desire to see spiritual, emotional, and physical healing. Traveling near and far, she encourages and inspires people (mostly women) through speaking engagements to know their identity and freedom in Jesus.

Rivera's transparent style marks her zeal for wanting people to experience God personally. She doesn't claim to be a theologian or have all the answers, but she does stand on the Bible as the final Word. Rivera is loyal, beautifully straightforward and desperate for all to know the freedom of Love Himself and walk in it daily. She's journeying messily through life just like everyone else. With a passion for revival, evangelism, and unity in the body of Christ, her greatest desire is to always point to the only One who matters, Jesus.

Connect

One of Rivera's greatest joys is connecting with her readers. Feel free to reach out through email, social media, or subscribe to her writings at RiveraDouthit.com or GoniaGlobal.org

- Instagram: riveradouthit

- Twitter: riveradouthit

- Facebook: Rivera Douthit

- Email: riveradouthit@gmail.com
  goniaglobal@gmail.com

- Mailing Address: Gonia Global
  99 Jackson St. #131
  Davidson, NC 28036

IF THIS BOOK MINISTERED TO YOU, PLEASE CONSIDER SHARING.

4 simple ways to share:

- Social media platforms, such as Facebook, Instagram, and/or Twitter.

- Recommend to your small group, reading club, classes, coworkers, and/or church.

- Pick up a copy for someone who would be encouraged by this message.

- Write a review on Amazon.

Made in the USA
Columbia, SC
15 June 2017